A JOURNEY TO HOLINESS

A JOURNEY TO HOLINESS

80 Years of Personal Prayers, Spiritual Inspirations, and Beliefs

RAYMOND JOHN COLVIN

Leonine Publishers
Phoenix, Arizona

Copyright © 2016 Raymond John Colvin

All rights reserved. No part of this book may be reproduced or transmitted in any form or by any means, electronic or mechanical, including photocopying, recording, or by any information storage or retrieval system now existing or to be invented, without written permission from the respective copyright holder(s), except for the inclusion of brief quotations in a review.

Scripture texts in this work are taken from the *New American Bible*, revised edition © 2010, 1991, 1986, 1970 Confraternity of Christian Doctrine, Washington, D.C. and are used by permission of the copyright owner. All Rights Reserved. No part of the *New American Bible* may be reproduced in any form without permission in writing from the copyright owner.

Published by Leonine Publishers LLC
Phoenix, Arizona
USA

ISBN-13: 978-1-942190-27-1
Library of Congress Control Number: 2016949879

Printed in the United States of America
10 9 8 7 6 5 4 3 2 1

Visit us online at www.leoninepublishers.com
For more information: info@leoninepublishers.com

Acknowledgments

I am grateful to all my religious and lay friends and family who have contributed to this book by their editing and contributions. I particularly appreciate their expertise and suggestions that have enabled me to remain faithful to the Catholic Magisterium.

And to my daughter Rosemary, who has so professionally reviewed this book and so aptly carried on her deceased mother's editing ability. Thank you for your hard work while keeping to your busy family schedule.

I especially want to thank my loving and spiritual wife, Kathy, for her continued support, patience, and encouragement throughout the years while I organized and wrote about my prayer life and my journey to eternity.

To my family and friends who over the years have heard me say during religious discussions, "It's in my book," thank you for your gracious Christian tolerance.

This is "my book."

What Is the Purpose of My Life?
(It is not complicated.)

It starts with understanding why you are here!

Why did God make me?

"God made me to know Him, to love Him, and to serve Him in this world, and to be happy with Him forever in Heaven."
Baltimore Catechism

Note: Once you get to know Him, then you will be able to love Him,

(How can you possibly love someone you don't know?)

and then you will be able to serve Him.

How simple is that?

See page 21 – "God's Plan for You"

Dedication

This book has been written especially for the people of the 21st century, my co-workers, friends and family, my children and grandchildren, who may have turned away from the Faith, or who no longer believe in God, or who have misplaced their spiritual priorities. For all of them, I dedicate this book. Through my daily prayers I place my hope and trust in God that they will all return to God for the benefit of their temporal life while here on earth, but mainly to attain their eternal happiness in Heaven.

I do understand that we are now living in a world and a culture that would not have been acceptable to my parents. While I dearly love everyone, regardless of their lifestyles or their activities, I do pray for them daily to change, and to become closer to God.

I am sure that my grandparents felt as I do today, witnessing the changes during their children's generation. The major difference of the cultural changes of this era is the extent to which people have turned away from God and replaced Him with the false gods of materialism, personal pleasures, anger, lies, pride, and vanity. These are serious violations of the first and most important of all commandments, to not have any strange gods (*or other priorities*) before God the Father.

I pray that God the Father provides the reader with an opportunity to use some of the prayer methods and spiritual resources that I have used throughout my lifetime. This may also help them attain a peaceful, wonderful, blessed life while on their journey to holiness that I am presently experiencing. I believe that my life has been guided and achieved totally through the protection, and blessings from, God the Father, Jesus His Son, the Holy Spirit, the Blessed Mother, and many saints. Additionally, I have been blessed with special intercessions from my guardian angel and the parents of the Blessed Virgin Mary: St. Anne and St. Joachim, who protect me physically, mentally, and spiritually each day.

The Author

God has blessed Raymond John Colvin with the gift of employment in a Catholic organization, where he is able to attend daily Mass and receive the Holy Eucharist. For all these gifts, but especially for the blessing of his wonderful family, including his saintly deceased wife and their six children, his many grandchildren, his great-grandchildren, and his wonderful, spiritual second wife, he is eternally grateful to God.

Colvin considers himself an "average" Catholic layman who, he believes, was not fortunate enough to receive a formal Catholic school education. He was blessed with a love for his Catholic faith which he manifested by his obedience to the Magisterium and the Holy Trinity. He is especially thankful to the Holy Spirit who has blessed him with a simple layman's understanding of how he should serve God. Throughout his lifetime, the Holy Spirit has provided him with special inspirations through the teaching of the Catholic Church and the examples of Jesus, the Blessed Mother, and the holy saints. The Holy Spirit has truly been the author's advocate and guide throughout his spiritual life, but especially in the writing of this book.

Mindful of all his blessings, Raymond takes seriously the Lord's admonition, "To those given much, much is expected." Luke 12:48

~ Rosemary (Colvin) Wynne,
daughter of the author

"Our progress in holiness depends upon God and ourselves. It depends on God's grace and on our will to want to be holy. We must have a real living determination to reach holiness."
Blessed Mother Teresa of Calcutta

Note: If you don't want holiness you will not get it, as God will not force it on you!

See page 14 – "Free Will"

Contents

Introduction
Page 1

CHAPTER 1
How and Why People Pray
Page 5

CHAPTER 2
Spiritual Motivations and Preparations
Page 27

CHAPTER 3
A Lifetime of Praying
Page 53

CHAPTER 4
Inspirations and Beliefs
Page 105

CHAPTER 5
Spiritual Observations and Resources
Page 143

Epilogue
Page 181

"Let us especially regret the smallest amount of time that we waste or fail to use in loving God."
St. John of the Cross

WHAT IS LOVE?

To love is to will the good of another, to live your life by serving someone other than yourself!

To love is to obey God by following His Son's example of the love that serves others.

It is God's will that we serve others.

Those who live only for themselves are serving the evil one.

See page 12 – "What Is Love?"

Introduction

The purpose of this book is to share my private spiritual life and my inspirations and beliefs. I wish to share these with all the people (Catholic and non-Catholic) of this generation and especially with the people who I love. My hope is that this will provide them with spiritual enlightenment through my prayer experiences, reflections, and inspirations that I received through the Holy Spirit.

The Holy Spirit, through Jesus and the Father, has blessed me with a healthy, peaceful, and wonderful blessed life. I have lived through eighty years of near-miss physical death experiences, served in the military during wartime, grew up during a depression and a world war, and have witnessed and experienced major technological and cultural changes. I have been extremely blessed and would like to share the personal prayers and inspirations that have helped me through these times.

"If on any particular day we do nothing more than give a little joy to a neighbor, that day will not be wasted. For we have succeeded in giving comfort to an immortal soul."
Blessed Contardo Ferrini

See page 23 – "Who Is a God-Pleasing Person?"

Notes

Many of the quotes throughout the book come from dogma and private revelation. The writer encourages the reader to research and verify his beliefs, observations, and inspirations through the use of the Bible, the Catechism of the Catholic Church, and "bishop-approved" Catholic publications.

(*According to the Catholic Church: dogma is mandatory to believe and private revelation is not mandatory.*)

Many of the author's observations about the Catholic faith are taken from well-known Bible quotes and passages, the Catechism of the Catholic Church, and from homilies at Masses. It is not within the scope of this book to provide a detailed explanation of each observation or belief. Rather, the author's intention is to describe in the most basic way the inspirations and spiritual beliefs which influenced the way he has prayed throughout his lifetime on his journey to holiness.

"Practice patience toward everyone,
especially toward yourself.
Never be disturbed because of your imperfections,
but always get up regularly after a fall."
St. Francis de Sales

See page 102 - "Our Dark Days Brings Us
Closer to God"

"Do you want to know one of the best ways
to win over people and lead them to God?
It consists in giving them joy and
making them happy."
St. Francis of Assisi

See page 117 – "God's Plan for Us"

CHAPTER 1

How and Why People Pray

"Prayer is the raising of the heart and mind to God."
St. John of Damascus

> An interviewer once asked St. John Paul II, "How does the Pope pray?" The Pope answered, "Ask the Holy Spirit!" This chapter describes the importance of the Holy Spirit in our prayer life, the need to understand the spiritual basics of our faith, and God's plan for us in order to fulfill His unwritten eleventh commandment:
> ***"To love and serve one another."***

How Do People Pray?

Have you ever watched someone praying in church and wondered what they were saying to God? What words were they using? To which of the three persons of the Holy Trinity were they praying? Were their prayers directed to God the Father, Jesus the Son, or the Holy Spirit? Were they talking to the Blessed Virgin Mary, to their guardian angel, their deceased relatives, or the saints? Were they asking for assistance with a personal problem, or asking for help on behalf of a family member or friend?

Also, have you ever seen people at Holy Mass and wondered what prayers they were saying right after receiving Holy Communion, when Jesus was spiritually and physically united with them for ten to fifteen minutes after receiving Him in the Holy Eucharist?

Pope Francis posed this question to the laity: "How do you pray?" Their answer was, "We give thanks to God and ask Jesus for help."

"Is that all you pray for—just asking for help and giving thanks?" The Holy Father challenged them. "You have ONLY two types of prayers? Do your prayers please God because He is so great, as we do in the Mass? As in the Sanctus, during the Mass? Could you not do that in your heart when you pray and are in His presence?" Then Pope Francis continued, "I ask another question—Do you adore God? Do you adore Him because He is the only God? Catholics should be like beggars when praying, and should praise and worship God. If you don't worship God you will have something else to worship."

The Holy Spirit's Inspirations When Praying

> *CCC 2664 There is no other way of Christian prayer than Christ. Whether our prayer is communal or personal, local or interior, it has access to the Father only if we pray "in the name of Jesus." The sacred humanity of Jesus is therefore the way by which the Holy Spirit teaches us to pray to God Our Father.*
>
> *(CCC = Catechism of the Catholic Church)*

The Holy Spirit assists us when we are praying and helps to bring our prayers to Jesus and to God the Father. When we pray, we need to understand that what we say to God is already known to Him. It is important to understand that God is spiritually present to us when we pray. We should be aware of His spiritual presence and let the Holy Spirit work within us as our advocate.

How would you like Jesus to be physically with you always as He was with the Apostles? To be able to talk to Him, question Him, and have Him as your friend, always at your side? How awesome would that be? We presently have that with the Holy Spirit!

> *CCC 2690 The Holy Spirit gives to certain of the faithful the gifts of wisdom, faith and discernment for the sake of this common good which is prayer (spiritual direction). Men and women so endowed are true servants of the living tradition of prayer.*

After the resurrection, Jesus returned to the Apostles and His mother in the upper room in Jerusalem. He told them that He would send the Holy Spirit to them when He went home to the Father. *(John 16:7)*

The Apostles were physically with Jesus for three years. During that time they could talk to Him, ask Him to explain His parables, and ask Him questions about the Father and how to serve others. We are able to call upon the Holy Spirit to do the same for us. All we have to do is call upon the Holy Spirit to enlighten us and to intercede for us to God the Father through Jesus.

> *CCC 2670 "No one can say 'Jesus is Lord' except by the Holy Spirit." Every time we begin to pray to Jesus it is the Holy Spirit who draws us on the way of prayer by His prevenient grace. Since He teaches us to pray by recalling Christ, how could we not pray to the Spirit too? That is why the Church invites us to call upon the Holy Spirit every day especially at the beginning and end of every important action.*
>
> *CCC 2672 The Holy Spirit, whose anointing permeates our whole being, is the interior master of Christian prayer. He is the artisan of the living tradition of prayer. To be sure, there are as many paths of prayer as there are persons who pray, but it is the same Spirit acting in all and with all. It is in the Communion of the Holy Spirit that Christian prayer is prayer in the Church.*

Pray Through the Holy Spirit to Jesus

In the Old Testament people prayed only to God the Father. They only knew the Father as God. Then Jesus came to earth for thirty-three years and taught mankind how to love, pray, and serve others. After Jesus returned to His Father, He sent us the Holy Spirit. How many people pray to the Holy Spirit in place of Jesus? How many pray to God the Father? How many pray to Jesus to intercede with the Father on their behalf? When Jesus healed people, when He prayed in the Garden of Gethsemane, who did He pray to? It was God the Father.

God has given us many resources to help us through our daily life. This includes our personal guardian angel who helps and protects us each day. St. Michael the Archangel helps protect us from Satan and his minions. The Blessed Mother intercedes for us with her Son Jesus, and also helps the saints intercede for us with Jesus. Additionally, the saints intercede on our behalf with Jesus and His Father.

Remember how the Apostles asked Jesus to save them when they feared their boat was going to sink? Jesus calmed the waters to save them. *(Matthew 8:24-27)* Today we can also call upon the Holy Spirit, our guardian angel, and St. Michael to help us in time of need or danger.

Do you pray through and with Mary to the Father? While He was on the cross Jesus gave us His mother through the Apostle John. *(John 19:27)* Just as Jesus sent us the Holy Spirit following His Ascension, He also left us with His mother. The Angel Gabriel foretold the importance Mary would have to Christians when

He proclaimed to her, "*Rejoice, O highly favored daughter, the Lord is with you, blessed are you among women.*" (*Luke 1:28*) Jesus' mother, Mary, is our advocate with her Son Jesus and the Father.

The Worldly Life vs. the Spiritual Life

To understand the nature of prayer we need to understand the levels of prayer—one is spiritual and the other human, or a worldly level. The human or worldly prayers are the words that we say and understand here on earth. Spiritual prayer exists in our next life. God and the saints reside in the next existence, while we reside in the present earthly life.

When you pray while in this earthly world you are communicating with someone (God the Father, Jesus, Mary, and the saints) in the spiritual world. It is important to understand the difference between the spiritual and the worldly. For example, here on earth we are bound by time (twenty-four hours a day, seven days a week, three hundred sixty-five days a year). There is not the same measurement of time in the spiritual world. It exists outside of time. There is no relationship to time when we pray to God for an intention. For example, if we pray to God and ask Him to cure the illness of a close family member, we of course would like them cured as soon as possible. But God might have another plan which requires them to suffer for a longer period of time—time in which they can draw closer to God through prayer. Spiritually, prayer has a higher importance than relieving worldly suffering. When we pray we need to mentally leave our worldly environment and enter into the spiritual world.

Sincerity is another element that brings us closer to the spiritual world. Sincerity is a form of love and a reflection of one's heart. Love cannot exist without sincerity. How sincere are we when we tell someone we love them? Sincerity, like love, cannot be measured by worldly standards. God measures our sincerity by His standards. It is said that God reads your heart, your soul, your intentions, and your sincerity.

> While words, posture, and actions are important while praying, the sincerity of prayer comes only through the heart. How sincere is your prayer? How heart-wrenching is it?

"A contrite and humbled heart, O God, you will not scorn." (Psalm 51:19)

God's Love for Us

"To love is to be transformed into what we love. To love God is therefore to be transformed into God." St. John of the Cross

God wants or needs nothing! He does not need our approval, thanksgiving, or sacrifices. When we do anything for God, He always returns it back to us. God shows us His love by returning all of the sacrifices that we make for Him. A powerful example of this kind of love is the great glory He bestowed on the Blessed Mother for the suffering she endured as she trusted in Him.

God loves those who love Him, and even loves those who do not love Him. In other words, God loves everyone! He created us for a purpose. While God is all loving, He is also just, and like a jealous lover, He wants a hundred percent of our love. He does not want our love shared with anyone or anything. The first and most important of the Ten Commandments is to not have strange gods before Him.

What Is Love?

"Children, let us love not in word or speech but in deed and truth." (John 3:18)

Love is going out of your way for someone or for something! Love is an action word. How much do you love and trust God? How much have you done for God? How faithful are you to your daily duties? How much time and effort do you give to God, your spouse, your children, your work, and your church? How much time do you spend in prayer? Do you allow God to talk to you? Do you pray slowly, pondering the words and what they mean?

When we pray the Our Father, we should try to visualize God our Creator, and speak humbly and slowly. Start your prayers by calling upon the Holy Spirit, asking for help in following Jesus' example of serving the Father. Give to God the first fruits of your day, and offer your work and prayers for His greater glory.

"Love, and do what you will. If you are silent, be silent out of love. If you speak, speak out of love. If you censure, censure out of love. If you forbear, forbear out of love. But love in your heart. Nothing but good can spring from that source." St. Augustine

> Love is the foundation of our faith. Before we can love Jesus, we must first know Him. Then we can serve Him. Love is doing something for someone which pleases him or her. Once we totally love someone, we can totally trust that person. We can now use the words spoken in the Chaplet of Divine Mercy to express this love... "Jesus I trust in you, Jesus I trust in you, Jesus I trust in you!"

We should open every prayer by thanking the Father for the blessings in our life. Ask the Holy Spirit for help in pleasing the Father. Ask Jesus for guidance and His intercession on your behalf. Additionally, ask the Blessed Mother for her intercession with her Son for the favors you are requesting. One of the quick prayers you can repeat over and over is *"Father, I Trust in You."*

"To love another person is to see the face of God." Victor Hugo, *Les Miserables*

Free Will

When God created man, the most important quality He gave him was free will. God could have created man to do everything that would please God. That would have made us mere robots, obeying His every command. Kings have subjects who do everything to please their king. God made man to freely and willingly know Him, love Him, serve Him, and be happy with Him in Heaven for all eternity. It is through prayer that we unite with our Creator to define our purpose in life as part of God's overall plan for His creation.

Prayer is wonderful because so many people from so many different backgrounds, through their free will, can come together to pray in church as a group, or individually. Men and women, young and old, rich and poor, healthy and suffering, businessmen and laborers, the highly educated and uneducated, are all talking to God in their own words.

There is also a common denominator among all people of free will who pray. They show their reverence to God first by blessing themselves *(which is calling upon the Holy Trinity)*, then by reciting prayers of thanks before asking God for a favor. They carry on a conversation with God, telling Him their problems, asking for His help, questioning Him about why He permitted something bad to happen. Sometimes they just want to give thanks for granting a request, or for the blessings of their life.

> Keep in mind that when you are talking to God, you are talking to your Creator, the one who gave you your life. You should always show respect and honor when talking to God!

How wonderful is diverse prayer and how powerful when believers, of their own free will, pray together in public for a common cause.

"For where two or three are gathered in my name, there I am in the midst of them." (Matthew 18:20)

We Cannot Pray or Work Our Way to Heaven

No one can become a saint in Heaven on their own. **Only God can make someone a saint if He wills it by granting His grace** (through His Son Jesus, who is the Chief Mediator of grace). **You need to want it and cooperate with Him.** All the prayers we say, or the good works we do, will not get us into Heaven unless God wills it. Prayer, along with good works, can become a method by which someone can become a saint. We will be judged on the sincerity of our work and prayers by Jesus our Judge. We should all strive to become saints. **(A saint is one who has already entered Heaven; every soul in Heaven is a saint.)** Our life goal should be to spend all eternity in Heaven with God, and we should remember this goal in our daily prayers.

God's Grace and Final Judgment

Only God the Father can give us grace. And it is only God the Father who can grant us entry into Heaven, after we have been judged by Jesus His Son. We cannot earn Heaven only by ourselves.

> *CCC 1996 Our justification comes from the grace of God. Grace is favor, the free and undeserved help that God gives us to respond to his call to become children of God, adoptive sons, partakers of the divine nature and of eternal life.*

All our deeds will be judged by Jesus, according to the love we had for others and how committed we were to our station in life—as a mother, father, son, daughter, religious, or layperson. We will be measured on how faithful we were to our commitments as a Christian. Were you a responsible Christian mother or father to your children? Did you set a good parental example? Were you a faithful spouse? Were you a faithful member of the Catholic Church, following the Magisterium and the laws of the Church? Were you a faithful employee, a faithful member of your community and your country? In His human nature, Jesus experienced everything that we do in life, except for sin. While God the Father knows all, He was never a human, so it is through His Son Jesus that we will be judged. Who better to judge us than Jesus who experienced human emotion, pain, and suffering? If the Father had not sent Jesus to us, there would be no Church, no Holy Eucharist, no Blessed Mother, no final judgment, and no redemption! Without Jesus, the gates of Heaven would not be open to us. Death would be real and forever. We must be grateful to Jesus and His mother who suffered so much to make our eternal future in Heaven possible.

What Can We Do to Please God?

There are three major responsibilities that we have in order to please God.

First, we must keep His Commandments.

Second, we must keep the Catholic Church's Five Precepts.
1. To attend Mass on Sundays and holy days of obligation, and rest from servile work on Sunday.
2. To observe the days of abstinence and fasting.
3. To confess our sins to a priest, at least once a year.
4. To receive our Lord Jesus Christ in the Holy Eucharist at least once a year, during Easter Season.
5. To contribute to the support of the Church.

(There are two additional actions that are encouraged)
- To obey the laws of the Church concerning Matrimony.
- To participate in the church's mission of the evangelization of souls *(the missionary spirit of the Church)*.

Third, we must be faithful to our duties according to our station in life.

> Nowhere are we required to recite a fixed number of prayers to please God.

God expects us to do all of our duties and responsibilities to the best of our abilities. St. Thérèse of Lisieux, according to the summation of her "Little Way," summed it up in this way: *"Do what you're supposed to do, when you're supposed to do it, in the way it's supposed to be done."*

Do not do anything half-heartedly, as this comes from Satan, who wants us to fail and become discouraged. Discouragement leads us away from the happiness of pleasing God to despair; despair manifests itself in the destructive behaviors of sex and drug abuse, alcoholism, sloth, anger, greed, and lying. These are the tools Satan uses to keep us away from God.

In order to keep His commandments, adhere to the precepts, and to remain faithful to our duties, we need to communicate with God for guidance and help. While most people know how to pray, most do not understand the process of prayer.

For example, who do you pray to? Most people would answer "to God." Yes, prayers ultimately do go to God, but to which of the three persons of the Trinity do you pray? God the Father, Jesus the Son, or to the Holy Spirit; or to all three in the Holy Trinity?

For whom or what do you pray? Yourself? Your family? Friends? The Church? Sinners? The souls in Purgatory? People who are suffering or in pain?

What media (newspapers, books, television, Internet, mobile phone, or other electronic equipment) do you or can you use to help your prayer life?

Do you regularly give thanks to God the Father for all the blessings and gifts He has given you, including your very life?

> Is there a formal process—a single correct way to pray to God? The simple answer is no. Prayer is a personal relationship with God, and as such there is no single correct way to pray.

What Is Prayer?

CCC 2559 Prayer is the raising of one's mind and heart to God or the requesting of good things from God.

CCC 2725 Prayer is both a gift of grace and a determined response on our part. It always presupposes effort. The great figures of prayer of the Old Covenant before Christ, as well as the Mother of God, the saints and he himself, all teach us this: prayer is a battle. Against whom? Against ourselves and against the wiles of the tempter who does all he can to turn man away from prayer, always away from a union with God. We pray as we live, because we live as we pray. If we do not want to act habitually according to the spirit of Christ, neither can we pray habitually in His name. The "spiritual battle" of the Christian's new life is inseparable from the battle of prayer.

> *CCC 2726 In the battle of prayer, we must face in ourselves and around us erroneous notions of prayer. Some people view prayer as a simple psychological activity, others as an effort of concentration to reach a mental void. Still others reduce prayer to ritual words and postures. Many Christians unconsciously regard prayer as an occupation that is incompatible with all other things they have to do: they "don't have the time." **Those who seek God by prayer are quickly discouraged because they do not know that prayer comes also from the Holy Spirit and not from them alone.** (Bold added)*

The forms of prayer are not only the words we use to talk to God and His family (Jesus, Mary, Joseph, the Holy Spirit, and the saints), it is also how we live our lives in His service. It's sincerely talking to God from our heart. Prayer is also keeping our Church obligations (going to Mass, receiving the sacraments, reciting daily prayers, observing holy days of obligation, etc.) We should make prayer the totality of all we do in life to serve God, our Creator.

Prayer is also a form of love and service to others. Without love and service, prayer cannot be effective. Prayer is a private spiritual communication with God, our Father and Creator. Everyone has their own prayer style and speaks to God through their heart and mind. We should understand who we are in relation to God, and who God is in relation to us.

God loves us so much that He gave us a third chance to please Him. After Adam and Eve, then Moses, He sent Jesus to show us examples of the equality, respect, and love He originally intended to give us through Adam and Eve.

God's Plan for You

In order to understand God's plan for each of us, we need to first know ourselves. Who are we? At what stage of life are we? Are we young, an adult, a senior, married, single, or a religious?

> God's plan is for you to be faithful to your state in life. He wants us to use the gifts He gave us—your knowledge and skills—to the best of your ability. Additionally, He wants us to help others become closer to Him.

For example, the first spiritual priority for you as a married parent should be saving your eternal soul. The second priority should be assisting your spouse to save their soul. The third priority is to teach your children about God and guide them in saving their souls. The fourth is to be an honest provider for your family; the fifth priority is to assist and support your Church; and the sixth is to help others save their souls.

(See page 167 – "The Fourteen Works of Mercy")

In summary, the most important consideration to achieve God's plan for you is to be faithful to your basic duties and responsibilities. Too many people lose sight of this and pursue "feel-good" activities in order to please God, but neglect their basic duties. An example of this would be spending too much time doing volunteer work while neglecting your spouse and family.

The Mission of My Life

John Henry Cardinal Newman shares his insight: *"God has created me to do Him some definite service. He has committed some work to me which He has not committed to another. I have my mission. I may never know it in this life, but I shall be told it in the next. I am a link in a chain, a bond of connection between persons. He has not created me for naught. I shall do good; I shall do His work. I shall be an angel of peace, a preacher of truth in my own place, while not intending it if I do but keep His commandments. Therefore, I will trust Him, whatever I am, I can never be thrown away. If I am in sickness, my sickness may serve Him, in perplexity, my perplexity may serve Him. If I am in sorrow, my sorrow may serve Him. He does nothing in vain. He knows what He is about. He may take away my friends. He may throw me among strangers. He may make me feel desolate, make my spirits sink, hide my future from me. Still, He knows what He is about."*

Who Is a God-Pleasing Person?

Certainly, someone who faithfully prays and serves God through his or her actions would be considered a God-pleasing person.

God's family consists of many different people. There are some who attend daily Mass, and faithfully say all their prayers (the rosary, the Divine Mercy Chaplet, morning and evening prayers, etc.). Yet these same people unfairly judge others and then hold grudges, gossip and criticize their family, friends, neighbors, or strangers, and who may not pray or attend Mass faithfully.

There are also people who do not attend church regularly but visit the sick, assist the needy, work in soup kitchens; perhaps they help their neighbors, friends, or family during stressful times. More importantly, they do not pass judgment, gossip or criticize others about how they practice their faith or live their lives.

Both types of people are part of God's family. Jesus showed us the way to please God by serving others and not passing judgment.

Jesus was asked why He ate with tax collectors and sinners. Jesus answered them; *"Those who are well have no need of the physician, but the sick do; I came not to call the righteous, but sinners."* (Mark 2:17)

Wouldn't it please God more if both groups went to church regularly, served others, avoided gossip, and did not pass judgment? Each of us will fall into both groups at some point in our lifetime. We will all participate in God-pleasing activities, and experience the dark days of selfishness, laziness, and self-absorption. Try to recite a short daily prayer in order to gain an understanding of how to achieve a good balance of prayer and service to others. An example of this could be:

> "Lord, grant that I may understand how I can pray to you by my good works as well as through the many words I use in prayer."

"This is the glorious duty of man, to pray and to love. To pray to God and to love God and to love your fellow man. If you pray and love, this is where a person's happiness lies."
St. John Vianney

(See page 168 – "The Three Eminent Good Works in Christianity")

Everything we have, from our knowledge and intellect to our very existence, are gifts from God. These gifts include our spouse, children, friends, possessions, skills, and employment. Practice gratitude and constantly thank God for all His gifts.

God's Plan Before and After Original Sin

God created Adam and Eve to share equality of dignity, respect, and love in their relationship as man and woman. They were to set an example for all future mankind, but this was lost after their original sin. After original sin, equality, respect, and love were wounded for all future generations of mankind. God gave man a second chance when He gave Moses the Ten Commandments as a guide to understand how we must love and respect one another.

How Much Does God Love Us?

Imagine how much parents love their children and want to protect them from physical harm. In order to keep them safe, they tell them, "Stay away from the hot stove; don't run out into the street; don't go near the fire; don't swim too far out," and so on. Loving parents also want to protect their children from any moral and spiritual harm, including violent or sexual television programming, computer games, and morally objectionable books.

As loving parents want to protect their children from any physical, mental, or spiritual harm, just imagine how much more our loving Father wants to protect us from harm. Most of all, God wants us to be happy with Him in Heaven for all eternity. And so, He gave us the Ten Commandments to guide and protect us from the moral and spiritual hazards of daily life. Today, mankind still struggles to understand and practice equality, respect, and love, even after being given the Ten Commandments and having Jesus show us the way.

The Eleventh Commandment

I personally propose an unwritten eleventh commandment:

"To love and serve one another."

Brothers and sisters: "Strive eagerly for the greatest spiritual gifts. But, I shall show you a still more excellent way. If I speak in human and angelic tongues, but do not have love, I am a resounding gong or a clashing cymbal.

And if I have the gift of prophecy, and comprehend all mysteries and all knowledge; if I have all faith so as to move mountains, but do not have love, I am nothing. If I give away everything I own, and if I hand my body over so that I may boast, but do not have love, I gain nothing.

Love is patient, love is kind. It is not jealous, it is not pompous, it is not inflated, it is not rude, it does not seek its own interests, it is not quick-tempered, it does not brood over injury. It does not rejoice over wrongdoing but rejoices with the truth. It bears all things, believes all things, hopes all things, and endures all things.

Love never fails. If there are prophecies, they will be brought to nothing; if tongues, they will cease; if knowledge, it will be brought to nothing. For we know partially and we prophesy partially but when the perfect comes the partial will pass away. When I was a child, I used to talk as a child, think as a child, reason as a child; when I became a man, I put aside childish things. At present we see indistinctly, as in a mirror, but then face to face. At present I know partially; then I shall know fully, as I am fully known. So faith, hope and love remain, these three; but the greatest of these is love." (1 Corinthians 12:31 - 13:13)

> Even after Moses added over 600 laws to the Ten Commandments to guide the Israelites, God found that His people lacked the love to understand the true meaning of His commandments. So God sent His Son Jesus to physically and spiritually teach and show His people love. **Jesus' and the Blessed Mother's suffering during His Passion and death are the ultimate examples of love.** Jesus conquered death and bought us our salvation with His LIFE and His LOVE.

CHAPTER 2

Spiritual Motivations and Preparations

"Those who pray are certainly saved; those who do not pray are certainly damned."
CCC 2744

> In this chapter I discuss praying to and through the Holy Spirit. I further discuss the importance of understanding the fundamentals of the Catholic faith before a Catholic layman can effectively employ the many types of prayers.

Prayer

Studies show that even non-believers pray. They pray when they talk through the spiritual world to a higher power. Prayer takes on many forms in addition to the spoken word. It may include singing, dancing, processing, reading sacred books, watching or listening to religious programming, working, and even keeping silent.

St. John of Damascus said, *"Prayer is the raising of the heart and mind to God. Our prayer becomes complete when it is engaged through the Holy Spirit and with the Holy Eucharist at which time our prayers are elevated into Heaven through our reception of Jesus in the Holy Eucharist."*

All prayers to the Father should end with, *"By Your will be done"* or *"Your will be done."* As Jesus said in the Garden of Gethsemane, *"My Father, if it is possible, let this cup pass from me; yet, not as I will, but as you will."* (Matthew 26:39)

For Catholics the most basic Christian gesture in prayer is the Sign of the Cross. To seal oneself with the Sign of the Cross is a visible and public "yes" to Him who suffered for us and has made God's love visible. By signing ourselves with the cross, we place ourselves under its protection. We hold the cross in front of us like a shield that will guard us in all the stresses of daily life and give us courage, especially during times of physical, mental, or spiritual danger.

Start every prayer by blessing yourself: *"In the name of the Father, and of the Son, and of the Holy Spirit. Amen."* In this prayer you are calling upon the Holy Trinity to begin your conversation with God. Do this especially upon awakening, before starting any prayers, before meals, and before going to bed. Making the Sign of the Cross has been described as dialing a telephone to speak to God!

Do you want to see God? Look around. What you see is what God made and it is good. God only makes what is good—the universe, the earth, people. Everything good is a reflection of God and His desires. All creation is for good. When you see Jesus, you see God. Jesus is pure love because only someone with pure love could suffer so much on our behalf.

"Give thanks always and for everything in the name of our Lord Jesus Christ to God the Father." (Ephesians 5:20)

Routine Prayer

Prayer throughout your lifetime will be erratic. There will be times of intense, urgent prayer; at other times, there will be dry periods and dark days when we will be less apt to pray.

During dark times, you should always force yourself to continue reciting your basic daily prayers: morning and evening prayers, prayers before meals, a rosary or Chaplet of Divine Mercy. These are the prayers we learned as children. We should feel guilty if we do not say them. They are there for our daily protection and guidance.

Some theologians and spiritual masters tell us that during your dry periods or dark days, God may be calling you to the "prayer of quiet." It is a common practice to set aside a special time during the day for prayer. You can use this time to talk with God the Father, Jesus, the Holy Spirit, the Blessed Mother, and the saints to request any special intentions or to give thanks for all the blessings or favors you received.

> Just as you set aside time to eat, sleep, wash, work, and spend time with your worldly family, you should formally schedule a daily visit with your spiritual family.

It could take place during a quiet activity like walking, sitting in a quiet room, or performing a non-hazardous activity. Be careful about praying in dangerous conditions which require your full attention such as driving a vehicle or operating machinery.

CCC 2698 The tradition of the Church proposes to the faithful certain rhythms of praying intended to nourish continual prayer. Some are daily, such as morning and evening prayer, grace before and after meals, the Liturgy of the Hours. Sundays, centered on the Eucharist, are kept holy primarily by prayer. The cycle of the liturgical year and its great feasts are also basic rhythms of the Christian's life of prayer.

Basic prayer activities include: morning and evening prayers; prayers before and after meals; attending Mass on Sunday and holy days of obligation; participating in the Sacrament of Penance/Reconciliation (confession) at least once a year; and to receive the Holy Eucharist (Holy Communion) during Easter time.

Additional activities where we can pray include: reciting a periodic rosary; attending a funeral, a First Communion, or a Confirmation Mass; participating in monthly reconciliation or penance; receiving Holy Eucharist weekly; attending occasional daily Mass;

participating in occasional Bible readings or study; participating in occasional adoration; helping others by joining community service groups such as the Altar Society or the Society of St. Vincent De Paul; and keeping up with timely Catholic news.

Advanced prayer activities include: praying a daily chaplet to the Divine Mercy, St. Michael, or your guardian angel; reciting a daily rosary; reading Scripture daily; participating in weekly adoration; regularly reading Catholic news; or attending group prayer services. Other activities include volunteering time for community activities; joining the Knights of Columbus, Women's Auxiliary of the Knights of Columbus, Legion of Mary, or other Catholic service organizations.

> *CCC 2699 The Lord leads all persons by paths and in ways pleasing to Him, and each believer responds according to his heart's resolve and the personal expressions of this prayer.* ***However, Christian Tradition has retained three major expressions of prayer: vocal, meditative, and contemplative. They have one basic trait in common: composure of heart.*** *This vigilance in keeping the word and dwelling in the presence of God makes these three expressions intense times in the life of prayer. (Bold added)*

Vocal Prayer

*CCC 2700 Through his word, God speaks to man. By words, mental or vocal, our prayer takes flesh. Yet it is most important that the heart should be present to him to whom we are speaking in prayer: **"whether or not prayer is heard depends not on the number of words, but on the fervor of our souls."** (Bold added)*

CCC 2701 Vocal prayer is an essential element of the Christian life. To His disciples, drawn by their master's silent prayer, Jesus teaches a vocal prayer, the Our Father. He not only prayed aloud the liturgical prayer of the synagogue but, as the Gospels show, He raised His voice to express His personal prayer, from exultant blessing of the Father to the agony of Gethsemane.

CCC 2702 The need to involve the senses in interior prayer corresponds to a requirement of our human nature. We are body and spirit, and we experienced the need to translate our feelings externally. We must pray with our whole being to give all power possible to our supplication.

Meditation Prayer

CCC 2708 Meditation engages thought, imagination, emotion, and desire. This mobilization of faculties is necessary in order to deepen our convictions of faith, prompt the conversion of our heart, and strengthen our will to follow Christ. Christian prayer tries above all to meditate on the mysteries of Christ, as in lectio divina or the rosary. This form of prayerful reflection is of great value, but Christian prayer should go further: to the knowledge of the love of the Lord Jesus, to union with Him.

Contemplative Prayer

What is contemplative prayer? St. Teresa of Avila answers: *"contemplative prayer, in my opinion, is nothing else than a close sharing between friends; it means taking time frequently to be alone with Him who we know loves us."*

That statement really sums up what praying is all about!

CCC 2709 Contemplative prayer seeks Him "whom my soul loves." It is Jesus, and in Him, the Father. We seek Him, because to desire Him is always the beginning of love, and we seek Him in that pure faith which causes us to be born of Him and to live in Him. In this inner prayer we can still meditate, but our attention is fixed on the Lord himself.

CCC 2718 Contemplative prayer is a union with the prayer of Christ in so far as it makes us participate in His mystery. The mystery of Christ is celebrated by the church in the Eucharist, and the Holy Spirit makes it come alive in contemplative prayer so that our charity will manifest it in our acts.

CCC 2724 Contemplative prayer is the simple expression of the mystery of prayer. It is a gaze of faith fixed on Jesus, and attentiveness to the Word of God, a silent love. It achieves real union with the prayer of Christ to the extent that it makes us share in His mystery.

People Who Have Influenced My Prayer Life

While walking to school, a grade school friend taught me how to pray during emergencies, especially upon hearing a fire truck, ambulance, or other emergency vehicle's alarm.

When I was in the Navy, I had a shipmate who would pray a rosary every evening in his bunk. I also joined a group of my shipmates to periodically pray the rosary at a local radio station when we were in port.

I watched my father praying on his knees at his bedside.

I watched my mother and mother-in-law praying to St. Anne at a shrine dedicated to her.

I watched my now-deceased wife pray on her knees for at least one hour before going to bed every evening.

I publicly prayed in churches, stadiums, and during public street processions with large groups of men from the Holy Name Society.

I have watched, and am always impressed, as I witness others publicly praying before meals in restaurants.

St. Edith Stein was known in religious life as Sister Teresa Benedicta of the Cross. One of the pivotal events in her life, which led to her conversion to the Catholic faith, occurred when she was still a practicing Jew. While a tourist in Frankfurt, Germany, she visited a Catholic cathedral and witnessed a woman kneeling, intensely praying in the silence of the church. She had never seen anyone praying alone, or outside of an organized prayer service. Something special happened to St. Edith Stein that day. Referring to what she saw, she wrote in her biography, "I could never forget that."

I am sure the woman praying at the cathedral never intended to inspire St. Edith Stein's conversion to the Catholic faith. The important message of this story is that we never know how our visible prayer activities will affect others. By setting a good example we can help others become closer to God. If we let Him, the Holy Spirit can use us in many ways. We just need to call upon Him daily, asking Him to *"Come Holy Spirit, come and let me be an instrument of God's plan."*

Accepting the Spiritual World

If you believe in God, then you must believe in God's spiritual world. If you believe in God's spiritual world, then you must believe that God's special spiritual powers exist beyond our human comprehension. For example, there are examples of saintly people who have lived for years without any food or water, existing solely on receiving daily the Holy Eucharist (Holy Communion). There are other saintly persons who were blessed with the phenomenon of bi-location: the supernatural ability to be in two places at once. There are also examples of the many miracles that happened at places such as Fatima and Lourdes.

God's same spiritual powers are at work during the Holy Mass when the bread and wine is turned into the body and blood of Jesus, known as transubstantiation. Medical specialists have analyzed some miraculously bleeding Hosts (Holy Communion) and found human tissue from the major muscle of the heart. Catholics actually receive the body and blood of Jesus, without physically tasting tissue or blood. When we receive the Holy Eucharist, we are actually taking Jesus into our bodies, and becoming part of our Lord through Jesus His Son. This action spiritually elevates our minds and hearts into Heaven where we can thank God the Father, Jesus, the Holy Spirit, the Blessed Mother, and all the saints for all they have done to lead us on our journey to Heaven.

> I have asked my grandchildren after they received their First Holy Communion: What did you receive today? Their answer was Jesus! I then asked, "What part of Jesus did you receive?" Of course, they looked perplexed and did not know what to answer. My loving response to them was, "You received part of His Heart!" (Receiving Jesus is also to receive His Heart.) I pray that they will never forget that they receive part of Jesus' Heart every time they receive the Holy Eucharist.

"May the Heart of Jesus in the Most Blessed Sacrament be praised, adored, and loved, with grateful affection, at every moment, in all the tabernacles of the world, even until the end of time. Amen."

While we do not understand the spiritual world, we accept it through our own faith and by God's gift of grace to us. Jesus tells us about the power of the spiritual world. *"If you had the faith of a mustard seed you can move mountains."* (Matthew 17:20)

We have the example of saints with great faith like Saint Padre Pio, who could read souls and minds, could heal the sick, and was capable of bi-location. We need to accept the existence of spiritual powers to be able to strengthen our faith.

Jesus has two natures—one divine and the other human. Jesus is physically real. We could have seen and touched Him if we had lived during His time on earth. By the power of the Holy Spirit, He entered this world born of the Blessed Mother and fathered by the Holy Spirit. When He returned to Heaven, He sent the Holy Spirit to us, trusting that the Holy Spirit would be our companion and guide.

Jesus was physically available to the Apostles and the thousands of people He came into contact with during His time on earth. We are blessed to have the Holy Spirit with us constantly, bringing us closer to the Father by helping us remain faithful to our station in life and assisting us in carrying the crosses we must bear.

Our Spiritual and Earthly Families

To achieve a better understanding of how to pray it would be helpful to recognize that we have both a spiritual family and a human family. As a gift from God, our biological earthly parents brought us into this world. It is God who starts all life and infuses each baby with a soul at the moment of conception. At the same time, He assigns a guardian angel to the conceived baby. Our guardian angel is then with us from the moment of our conception until our last breath.

"Every soul is committed to an angel at the moment when it is united with a body." St. Anselm

"For he commands his angels with regard to you, to guard you wherever you go." (Psalm 91:11)

"The Angels are the shepherds of our souls. Not content with bringing our messages to God, they also bring God's messages to us. They nourish our souls with their delightful inspirations as well as their divine communications." St. John of the Cross

Earthly parents can provide their children with physical necessities, love, guidance, and protection. But they also need to work together with their spiritual partners, God who created their baby, and the saints in Heaven. When we pray, we have a spiritual family to pray with and for us.

All prayers ultimately go to God the Father through His Son Jesus, who is our spiritual and earthly brother, and through the Holy Spirit! In the same way, you can ask the Blessed Mother, Saint Joseph, and the saints to go to Jesus to ask God the Father to grant our petitions. Always end all prayers for petitions or favors with, *"and let God the Father's will be done as He knows what is best for me."*

If we accept and understand the depth of our godly family, then we should also accept that every human being is our brother or sister in our godly family, as we are all related through Adam and Eve—we were all created by God. This is why we should love everyone as a relative, regardless of our differences and in spite of how difficult it may be. If we could only comprehend and understand how we will all meet as God's children, brothers and sisters in the next life, we might be more tolerant and accepting of our human weaknesses and failings in this life!

"Judge not, that you be not judged. For with the judgment you pronounce you will be judged, and the measure you give will be the measure you get!" (Matthew 7:1-2)

Are the children that I fathered really special? Are they any better than other children of the world? Should I pray more intensely for my children than for other hurting children outside of my family? If you believe that we are all related as spiritual brothers and sisters, then we should love and pray for everyone equally!

Different Forms of Prayer

The only types of prayers or religious activities required by the Catholic Church include: Baptism; attending Mass on Sundays and holy days of obligation; annual confession; observing the days of abstinence and fasting; Easter Duty (receiving Holy Eucharist at least once during the Easter season which lasts from Easter through Pentecost).

These are additional times of prayer:
- The Sacraments of Marriage, Holy Orders, and Anointing of the Sick
- Attending Holy Mass during the week
- Prayers before the exposed Blessed Sacrament
- Group prayer *(where two or more faithful pray together)*
- Prayers during sleep difficulty
- Prayers when experiencing medical problems
- Prayers at the time of death
- Prayer in private quiet times
- Liturgy of the Hours
- Prayers before Jesus in the tabernacle
- Prayers before a crucifix
- Prayers to the Blessed Mother
- Prayers to the saints for intercessions
- Prayers to our guardian angel
- Prayers for the deceased in Purgatory or to those in Heaven

"*Silence exists so that we might speak and listen to God. And it is in silence that God communicates His graces to us.*"
St. Vincent de Paul

In times of silence I pray the following prayer:

"Help me, Father, to appreciate the value of silence in my life so that I may set aside a few minutes each day to think about all You have done for me for my salvation. Give me the opportunity to speak and listen to You and give You thanks for all You have blessed me with."

Opportunities for Prayer

There are many opportunities for prayer: while reading; during quiet time; watching religious programming on television or online; praying with a priest or family members; reciting a rosary at church before or after Mass; in bed at night; at work; while walking, and so on.

Jesus said, *"Some evils can be driven out only by prayer and fasting. There is a power that comes from joining our body with our heart and soul." (Matthew 17:21)*

Prayer that is combined with fasting or other forms of penance or sacrifice is more powerful. The denial of physical pleasures coupled with prayers make them more intense, as this demonstrates conviction to prayer. For example, by getting up early in the morning to pray, when you would rather stay in bed to sleep another hour, demonstrates your commitment to your prayer life.

Note: We must not participate in excessive fasting or sacrifice. Satan wants you take on more then you should "for God," because when we do this, we risk burn-out and discouragement which can cause us to give up these activities entirely.

> We need to exercise moderation in everything we do, because moderation gives balance to our life, including our prayer life.

Even monks and nuns, who live a cloistered life in daily prayer for others, must take time to sleep, eat, and rest. They cannot pray twenty-four hours a day, although they can offer all they do, including eating and sleeping, to God as a form of prayer, which we can also do.

Many holy, well-meaning people overdo their religious activities. They love God so much that they are overly active in their church, join many prayer groups, and participate in social welfare programs. Excessive participation and volunteerism may lead to neglect of their health, family, or basic obligations. This can ultimately lead to discouragement, and family or health problems. These problems can turn a faithful soul away from God.

> *"Be very careful to preserve your health. The devil employs a trick to deceive good souls. He incites them to do more than they are able, in order that they may no longer be able to do anything."* St. Vincent de Paul

Upon Waking in the Middle of the Night

God may want to talk to you when you can't get to sleep! Remember, prayer is talking to God. When you were young, you generally did all the talking—telling God what you wanted Him to do for you. As we mature, we learn to listen to what God wants us to do for Him.

"Eli said to Samuel, 'Go to sleep, and if you are called, reply, "Speak Lord for your servant is listening",' and when Samuel went to sleep and the Lord came, Samuel answered, 'Speak Lord, for your servant is listening.'" (1 Samuel 3:9-10)

Therefore, make it a practice to ask God to speak to you when you awaken in the middle of the night.

Spiritual Motivations and Preparations

> "Speak, Lord, for your servant is listening."

Maybe you didn't spend enough time with God during the day and there is something He wants to tell you. Maybe He just wants your company in the middle of the night, or perhaps He wants to be alone with you in silence.

If you experience difficulty finding the words to use to pray, keep it simple, as St. Francis did. Especially if you are in pain or depressed.

St. Francis of Assisi prayed throughout the night just repeating over and over, *"My Jesus, mercy!"*

CCC 2743 It is always possible to pray: the time of the Christian is that of the risen Christ who is with us always, no matter what tempests may arise. Our time is in the hands of God.

CCC 2744 Prayer is a vital necessity. Proof from the contrary is no less convincing: if we do not allow the Spirit to lead us, we fall back into the slavery of sin. How can the Holy Spirit be our life if our heart is far from Him?

> *Nothing is equal to prayer; for what is impossible it makes possible, what is difficult, easy.... For it is impossible, utterly impossible, for the man who prays eagerly and invokes God ceaselessly ever to sin. Those who pray are certainly saved; those who do not pray are certainly damned.*

Give God Your Best, Not Your Leftovers!

Every morning promise God you'll give Him your best. During your evening prayers, tell God how you tried to give Him your best, and how tomorrow you will try to do better.

> You are at a major point of conversion in your prayer life when you stop telling God what you want and start trusting God to give you what you need.

It is human nature to tend to tell God what to do and what we need, rather than asking God what He wants us to do for Him.

St. Ignatius of Loyola instructed us, *"to seek the greater glory of God in everything that we do."* To seek the will of God is the first level of conversion. The next level of conversion is to do the will of God. To do His will it is necessary to know His will. We must know His Ten Commandments and follow the example of His Son Jesus.

> *CCC 2664 There is no other way of Christian prayer than Christ. Whether our prayer is communal or personal, vocal or interior, it has access to the Father only if we pray "in the name of Jesus." The sacred humanity of Jesus is therefore the way by which the Holy Spirit teaches us to pray to God the Father.*

Therefore, all prayers should go through Jesus to God the Father. Jesus sent us the Holy Spirit, who continues Jesus' examples of love. When we pray to the

Blessed Mother we ask her to bring our prayer to her Son, who will bring it to God the Father. When we pray to a saint, we ask the saint to bring our request to Jesus who will then bring it to God the Father.

All Favors and Prayer Requests are Only Granted by God the Father Who has the Final Approval.

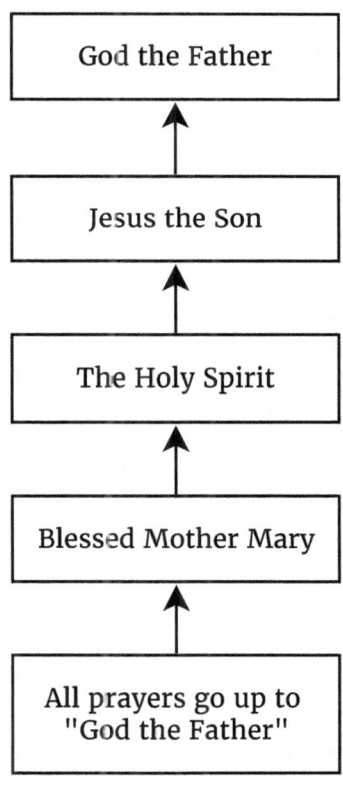

> *Some of my most powerful prayers to God the Father happen when I call upon Him through the saints in Heaven, or the future saints in Purgatory and to the Holy Spirit, who then goes to Jesus who goes to the Father. Also, when the saints bring our requests to the Blessed Mother, she intercedes for us directly with her Son, who then goes directly to God the Father.*

"To serve God is to reign." St. Antonius

> CCC 2670 "No one can say 'Jesus is Lord' except by the Holy Spirit." **Every time we begin to pray to Jesus it is the Holy Spirit who draws us on the way of prayer by His prevenient grace.** Since He teaches us to pray by recalling Christ, how could we not pray to the Spirit too? That is why the Church invites us to call upon the Holy Spirit every day, especially at the beginning and the end of every important action. (Bold added)

The Church invites us to call upon the Holy Spirit every day, especially at the beginning and the end of every important action. The personal prayer that I use is: *"Come Holy Spirit, and help us to do the Father's will."*

The Blessed Mother and Our Spiritual Family

Why pray to God through Mary?

St. Bernard wrote, "As you struggle through the stormy sea of life, do not turn away from Mary, Star of the

Sea. If the winds of temptation blow your little boat, or if you are headed toward the rocks of suffering, look at the star—called Mary! If you are tossed by the waves of ambition or envy, look at the star—called Mary! If anger or greed rocks the little boat of your heart, look at Mary! If you are getting discouraged because of your sins, think of Mary! In dangers and difficulties, remember Mary—call Mary! **Do not let her name be far from your lips. Keep the thought of her fixed in your heart! She will keep you from losing your way. She will protect you so you have nothing to fear. She will guide you to Jesus, your Savior!"**

Just as sailors who may be caught in a storm that use the stars to chart their course, we can look to Mary as our "Star," who keeps us on the path that Jesus marked out for us. If we get off course in our life, we can look to Mary and she will guide us back to Jesus and His Church.

At the wedding feast at Cana, Mary felt compassion for the bride and groom as they ran out of wine for their guests. *Her human motherly instincts make Mary sensitive to all our human problems.* If we ask her, she will go to her Son Jesus, to help us. But, as she said to the servers at the wedding feast, "Do as He says." It is important that we do what Jesus tells us, even if we do not like or understand what He tells us.

The Blessed Mother stated that many people need her help. She said, *"Just let them ask me."* She is waiting for our requests that she will take to Her Son to bring to God the Father.

The next time you need help from God, go to Jesus' Mother. *You can also go to Jesus' grandmother and grandfather* (Mary's mother and father, St. Anne and St. Joachim). Additionally, all the saints in Heaven are our brothers and sisters, so we can also go to them for help. In the Bible, when Jesus referred to His brothers and sisters, the reference was to His spiritual family members, not earthly brothers and sisters. (Matthew 12:49, Luke 8:21, Mark 3:34)

> What a wonderful spiritual family we have! A family that prays together is a powerful family. Call upon your spiritual family in time of need. Remember, you are never alone. Your spiritual family is always with you and waiting to help, if you only ask.

For additional help, you can call upon your brothers and sisters in Purgatory, who are the future saints in Heaven! Their prayers are very powerful as they suffer in purification. While they are in Purgatory, they cannot pray for themselves. If you pray for them, they will remember you when you are in Purgatory and cannot pray for yourself. It is not a foregone conclusion that you will definitely spend time in Purgatory. There are some people who will go straight to Heaven—and we might be surprised who they might be!

Consider the evolution of prayer. Our ancestors looked up to the sky, or to a mountain, and prayed directly to God. Today we can pray to God with the help of different types of media resources—books, newspapers, magazines, television, computer, and smart phones, to name a few. These tools can provide us with additional ways of how we can pray to God.

The following is a diagram of my Spiritual Family to whom I regularly pray as I give thanks and request favors or guidance.

My Spiritual Family

My Heavenly Family Who I Regulary Pray To and Through to God the Father

Blessed Mother	St. Joseph	Guardian Angel
St. Anne	St. Raymond	Deceased Wife
St. Joachim	Deceased Priests	Souls in Purgatory
St. John	Deceased Family Members	Deceased Friends
St. Michael the Archangel		Mother Mary Angelica

My Guardian Angel

My guardian angel knows me better than I know myself. He knows everything about me (everything that God wants him to know): my physical condition, my mental state, my level of sincerity, and my feelings. He knows how to protect me, guide me, and lead me.

My angel guardian is a true friend and a marvelous gift from God to help and protect me on my journey to holiness!

The Sincerity of Prayer

How would you feel if you invited people to visit you, but during their visit that person didn't spend any time talking to you? How would you feel if they stared out the window, answered phone calls, constantly checked for and answered text messages, or watched television, paying no attention to you? How would you feel about the sincerity of their feelings for you?

When you pray to God, do your thoughts wander? How do you think God feels when you come to church (His home) and are preoccupied with endless distractions? How do you think He feels when you don't give Him your full attention?

Is it any different when you are praying? How sincere is your prayer? If you have a major health problem, you will most likely be sincere, praying "Please God, save me. Let me live!" As the Apostles' prayers were sincere when they asked Jesus to save them from drowning during the sudden storm, we are sincere and child-like in our prayers when we encounter serious problems. Why is it when things are going well in our lives we do not pray with the same urgency or sincerity? Human nature is to blame. Our prayers have much more value when we pay attention to God and give Him thanks and honor for all He has given us.

St. Thomas Aquinas' sister once asked her brother, *"What must I do to be a saint?"* His answer was, *"Will it, want it, desire it."*

While we honor well-known saints for what they accomplished in life, we must remember that their deeds were possible only through the grace of God, through Jesus and the Holy Spirit. The saints never accomplished anything solely through their own abilities!

The great spiritual advisor Thomas Merton, in his earlier years, said that, *"Prayers like the Our Father, and the Hail Mary, are often a great way to lead you to prayer."*

Whenever you have doubts about how to please God, always ask yourself, *"What would Jesus or the Blessed Mother do in this situation?"* In that you will find your answer.

> *"The first task of love is to acknowledge before God that we belong to Him. We owe our lives to Him alone. Hence, our hearts must be free of everything that concerns anyone else."* St. Zeno

> *"Our true worth does not consist in what human beings think of us. What we really are consists in what God knows us to be."* St. John Berchmans

CHAPTER 3

A Lifetime of Praying

"If you really want your love for Christ to grow and last, then you must be faithful to prayer."
St. John Paul II

In this chapter I describe how my prayer life developed and provide examples of my personal prayers as I matured from a young child through adulthood and into my senior years.

Additionally, I share the exact words and prayers I use to pray throughout the day. I detail my daily and weekly private prayers and their accompanying actions, and share how they have gotten me through the occasional dark days and dry periods when my prayer life has been challenged.

A Brief Overview of How My Personal Prayer Life Evolved Over Eighty Years

As an Infant/Child *(0–6 years old: During the 1930s Great Depression and the beginning of World War II)*

My mother taught me the basic prayers and brought me to our parish church for Sunday Mass with my father, and on short visits to church during the week. During these years my mother taught me to stop by a church to visit Jesus because He was lonely and wanted some company.

During Childhood *(6–12 years old: In public schools during World War II and postwar recovery)*

I attended weekly Mass. (My mother taught me to never miss an obligatory Mass because it was a very serious sin and it would make God sad.) I regularly recited the Our Father, Hail Mary, and evening prayers. I prayed with my family before holiday meals. After I made my First Holy Communion, I went to monthly Confession. I visited Catholic shrines in the United States and Canada during vacations with my family.

As a Youth/Teen *(12–18 years old: Attended public high school during the Korean War)*

I went to weekly Mass and prayed with other teens in church. I recited the rosary with a high school female friend and her family, and prayed more frequent prayers to the Blessed Mother, especially during times of temptation. As a youth, I feared punishment from God if I committed a serious sin. Throughout my youth, fear kept me faithful to my Catholic obligations. As I grew older, I realized that I loved God and did not want to offend Him. Rather than fear God, I did not want to disappoint Him.

Teen/Adult Years (*18–23 years old: Attended public college, then left to join the Navy during the Korean War*)

During these years, I prayed the rosary more frequently, and always carried rosary beads in pocket. I recited a daily rosary especially at night while in the Navy. I also recited rosaries on a local radio station with some of my shipmates. I attended religion classes for converts while in the Navy to learn more about the Catholic faith. I visited Catholic shrines and churches during my Navy travels around the world.

As a Young Married Adult (*23–35 years old: I returned home from the Navy, married a holy, spiritual woman, and was blessed with six children in six years.*)

During this time, I visited churches and shrines in the United States and Canada while on my honeymoon and family vacations. I was active in parish church activities, and became a member of the Holy Name Society and Knights of Columbus. I became involved in parish fundraising, and assisted my pastor with church activities including serving as a lector at Mass. I opened my house, and befriended and socialized with priests from a local monastery (one priest was a close member of my family.) I continued to visit Catholic shrines on family vacations and occasionally on weekends, and to expose my children to the religious life. As a young father of young children, I prayed regularly to St. Joseph and the Blessed Mother (the Virgin Mary) for guidance and help.

Adult Years *(35–60 years old: Raised my children into adulthood. They all married and began raising their own families.)*

My holy wife and I educated our children by expressing examples of love and respect for each other at home, and by enrolling them in the Catholic school system while exposing them to other activities associated with the Catholic Church. I increased my visits to churches and shrines, occasionally attending daily Mass and one hour of Adoration. I also continued to assist my parish pastors and bishops in times of need and special activities. I served on parish councils and the board of directors for an order of nuns. I served as a management consultant for their schools, a nursing home, a Catholic hospital, and I chaired their fundraising activities. I served as president of the Holy Name Society for more than thirty years and was president of the Holy Name district, which included twenty-eight parishes. My duties included organizing annual conferences and retreats.

I prayed regularly for guidance as a grandparent and for my grandchildren to St. Anne and St. Joachim. I increased the amount of time I spent watching religious television programming (especially on EWTN) and religious movies about saints.

As a Mature Adult *(60–75 years old: A time of change in which my first holy wife was called to Heaven. I remarried a spiritual woman several years later to help me on my journey to holiness.)*

I attended daily Mass and made regular visits to the Blessed Sacrament. I started a formal private prayer life, and prayed the rosary and Chaplet of Divine Mercy with my wife daily. I increased my understanding of and devotion to the faith under the guidance of my spiritual advisor. I set up a formal prayer space in my home where I increased the amount of "quiet talking time" I spend with God the Father, Jesus, the Holy Spirit, St. Anne and St. Joachim, my guardian angel, and patron saints. I spent more time studying the Bible.

Senior Years *(75+ years old)*
I have increased my formal prayer time and activities, and the amount of time I spend talking to and seeking support and guidance from God the Father, Jesus, the Holy Spirit, my guardian angel, St. Anne and St. Joachim. I have increased my Bible studies. Each day, I watch Holy Mass on the Eternal Word Television Network (EWTN) paying attention to the readings and the homily for the day. I also attend daily Mass at work or at one of my local churches. *(Since 1991 I have been blessed to be affiliated with Mother Angelica's Eternal Word Television Network).*

Note: *I started working as a child when I was eight years old delivering newspapers, shining shoes, and working odd jobs before I went into the military and have continued working until this present time. I have worked all my life and have been blessed with good health and rarely missed a day of work. (Even after a triple-bypass heart operation, I missed only three days).*

The Value of Time When Praying

> The most valuable gift that we have in life is time. It never stops nor can we save it. Time is the bridge between Heaven and earth.

Time as we know it only exists in this earthly life, not in the final spiritual world. Therefore, the most precious gift we can give to the Father or the saints is our time in one of the many forms of prayer. The most important time of prayer is in the present moment. The past is gone; we can never get it back. The future is something we can only imagine, and for which there is no guarantee.

The best form of prayer is to set a good example. Do your very best, regardless of the task and your station in life. Doing your very best is a way to give thanks for all the suffering Jesus endured on our behalf. God has blessed each of us with special personal unique skills and talents. Imagine how disappointed God is when we don't use His gifts to the best of our ability.

Time spent in silence is another form of effective prayer. There are untold benefits to be gained by sitting in silence at home or before the Blessed Sacrament in church. Open your mind to God. Let Him inspire you. The inspirations which involve helping others come from God. (Inspirations that are self-centered or self-serving are not generally from God.)

Praying Through and To the Saints

Praying through and to a saint is like having an advocate representing you before God.

Remember the story of the centurion with a servant who asked Jesus to cure him? The centurion was his servant's advocate.

But, when the centurion said to Jesus, "Lord, I am not worthy to have you come under my roof, but only say the word, and my servant will be healed."... Jesus was so impressed with the centurion's faith that He said, "Truly, I say to you, not even in Israel have I found such faith." (Matthew 8:8,10)

Also in the Bible there is the story about the men who lowered their friend through the roof for Jesus to cure. They were his advocates.

> Imagine having many saintly advocates in Heaven representing you before God.

Think about having a saint you admire as your personal intercessor, advocate, and lawyer before God. This saint will work for you, present your causes and requests, and plead for mercy on your behalf for the times you failed to live up to God's expectations.

Think of a saint with whom you feel some connection. Talk to him or her. Tell the saints of your needs. Ask them to speak to Jesus and the Father on your behalf. As you would with any person you admire, look up information about them. Everyone likes to have their friends know about them and their experiences. Show that kind of respect to the saints you converse with and ask them to be your friend and advocate.

> How often can you pray to God during the day? Five, ten, twenty times? Your saintly advocates work for you twenty-four hours a day, seven days a week, three hundred sixty-five days a year.

What can you possibly give to God who has everything and is everything? *"I heard the voice of the Lord saying: Whom shall I send? And who will go for us? Then I said: 'here I am, send me!'" (Isaiah 6:8)*

"We ask what we might offer to God. Offer yourself! What does God expect from you except yourself?" St. Augustine

Jesus said to His disciples: *"In praying, do not babble like the pagans, who think that they will be heard because of their many words. Do not be like them. Your Father knows what you need before you ask Him." (Matthew 6:7)*

Prayer is more than just words. Prayer is a combination of desire, sincerity, and dedication to please the Father, while giving thanks for everything He has given you. Always start your prayers by first humbling yourself and giving thanks.

The Prayer That Jesus Taught Us

The only prayer that we know that comes directly from God Himself is the "Our Father," the prayer that Jesus taught us.

The Our Father provides the framework for how we should pray.

"Our Father, who art in Heaven." This is our greeting for the Father, recognizing His Majesty in Heaven.

"Hallowed be thy name," is the way we honor and adore God.

"*Thy kingdom come, thy will be done on earth as it is in Heaven.*" We pledge our obedience to and trust in God.

"*Give us this day our daily bread.*" We ask God to bless this day and provide for our physical and spiritual needs. We also thank Him for the Eucharist, our living Bread.

"*And forgive us our trespasses as we forgive those who trespass against us.*" We ask forgiveness for those that we have hurt, or those we failed to help (sins of omission!) in their time of need. Just as we forgive others who have hurt us.

"*And lead us not into temptation, but deliver us from evil. Amen.*" We ask God to spare us from the heavy crosses that might tempt our faith, and to protect us from Satan and his followers.

Growth of Prayer in the Stations of Life

> *CCC 2685 The Christian family is the first place of education in prayer. Based on the sacrament of marriage, the family is the "domestic Church" where God's children learn to pray "as the Church" and to persevere in prayer. For young children in particular, daily family prayer is the first witness of the Church's living memory as awakened patiently by the Holy Spirit.*

Serious prayer requires an understanding of our responsibilities, and to whom we are responsible. Who are we responsible for? What obligations do we have in our station of life?

> Every human brought into this world will suffer and eventually die. When we die, we will leave this world and spiritually go into the next phase of life. Our body will die, but our soul will live forever.

Many people have life insurance policies to provide for their loved ones in the event of their death. How many people have thought about a spiritual life insurance plan for all eternity?

God Never Sends Anyone to Hell

God always gives us choice through our free will. How we live our life on earth and how we carry out God's will for us will determine where we will spend eternity.

"Not everyone who says to me, 'Lord, Lord', shall enter the kingdom of Heaven, but he who does the will of my Father, who is in Heaven." (Matthew 7:21)

"Everyone then who hears these words of mine and does them will be like a wise man who built his house upon rock!" (Matthew 7:24)

"And on everyone who hears these words of mine and does not do them will be like a foolish man who built his house upon sand!" (Matthew 7:26)

> There is a popular saying that "the road to hell is paved with good intentions!" (Having good intentions is not doing the will of God! But it is taking the lazy way of only thinking about doing God's will, and not actually doing it!)

The Importance of a Routine Prayer Life

Throughout life, our goal should be to spend eternity with God in Heaven. In this pursuit we should be like athletes training for the Olympics. To ensure peak performance, they work with their coach and practice, practice, practice. We should follow their example, constantly praying and talking to God so that we may become like a world-class athlete.

Routine prayer can be repetitive when said over and over again. But you should constantly repeat those prayers to perfect and remember them, just as you must practice your exercises to improve your physical and mental skills.

> Show God your love by going out of your way for Him. Get up early to say a rosary. Go to an hour of adoration. Visit a church or a shrine. Love is an action word. Go out of your way for God and spend some time with Him if you truly love Him.

St. John Paul II's biographer said he was amazed to find out how often the Holy Father prayed. When he prayed, the pope lay prostrate, on his face, before

Jesus who was present inside the private tabernacle in the pope's chapel. He prayed humbly, like a beggar.

If we are to be co-heirs with Jesus Christ in His Kingdom, we must also share in His suffering and Passion as well. He wants us to consider that the suffering we experience in our lifetime is a small price when compared to the glory of Heaven.

St. Catherine of Siena said, *"It is Heaven all the way to Heaven."*

If you really trust in God, you will stay in the present moment and not worry or be concerned over what has happened in the past or what might happen in the future! Remember this warning from God: *"You fool! This night your life will be required of you!"* (Luke 12:20)

St. Paul tells us that *"On some days, we may be too distracted to pray. Periods of anger, depression, illness or reason may blind us to God's presence."*

Even so, St. Paul encourages unceasing prayer, because *"the Spirit too comes to the aid of our weakness; for we do not know how to pray as we ought, but the Spirit itself intercedes with inexpressible groaning. And the one who searches hearts knows what is the intention of the Spirit, because, the Holy Spirit intercedes for the holy ones* **(that's us)** *according to God's will."* (Romans 8:26-27)

A Suggested Daily Prayer Routine

Start each day by asking God's blessings for your family, friends, and all who are suffering physically, mentally, and spiritually. Pray for the suffering souls in Purgatory. Remember that the priests and religious who are in Purgatory don't have biological children who pray for them, and they are in special need of our prayers. We owe them an enormous gratitude for bringing us Jesus in the Holy Eucharist throughout our lives! **Pray for priests!**

(See page 171 – "A Prayer for Our Pastor and Shepherd")

Include in your morning prayers a request for help and forgiveness. This prayer can be as simple as *"Bless all my activities and forgive my selfishness and all my sins of omission."* Likewise, include this same petition in your evening prayers, asking for God's grace to assist you to fulfill His plan for you.

There will be times when we will say many prayers throughout the day, and times of fewer prayers. The intensity of our prayer life will vary with our circumstances. The basic prayers should be the cornerstone of our prayer life. We should be committed to saying our basic prayers each day, regardless of the difficulty it presents.

You can supplement your basic prayers with prayers from EWTN's radio or television programs. You may also participate in the daily family prayer broadcast on EWTN, recited before the daily Mass worldwide. **When you do this, you are praying in union with millions of people across the world.** This is truly a powerful prayer!

> Our prayer life is strengthened through frequent attendance at Mass and by receiving the Holy Eucharist. In the Lord's Prayer we say: "Give us this day our daily bread." At Mass we receive Jesus' words through the Gospels and the homily, in addition to the Holy Eucharist, as our daily "bread."

When we pray before meals in public places, we are acknowledging our God. Jesus said, *"If you deny me before others, I will deny you before my heavenly Father!"* (Matthew 10:33) Don't be ashamed of blessing yourself and publicly giving thanks to God and to ask for His blessing.

St. Monica is the model for persistent prayer that never quits. After seventeen years of praying for her sinful son, she was rewarded with his conversion. He ultimately became St. Augustine and a doctor of the Church.

Fasting and abstaining from eating meat on Fridays requires sacrifice and as such, is a form of prayer.

Prayer doesn't need to be lengthy to be effective. Praying the Divine Mercy Chaplet takes only seven to eight minutes. Praying the rosary takes less than 25 minutes.

Get into the habit of praying short inspirational prayers throughout the day. Say: *"Thank You, Jesus"*; *"Thank You, Father"*; *"Thank you, Blessed Mother"*; *"My Guardian Angel, protect me"*; and, *"O Sacrament most Holy, O Sacrament divine. All praise and all thanksgiving be every moment Thine."* When passing a cemetery, you can say, *"Eternal rest grant unto them, O Lord, and* let perpetual light shine upon them." You may also add, "May their souls and all the souls of the faithful departed, through the mercy of God, rest in peace. Amen." If you see a person who is disabled or in pain, you can pray: "My Jesus, have mercy on him."

How we pray is what we believe!

The Most Formal Prayer Is the Holy Mass

The prayer of the Mass was passed down from Jesus at the Last Supper, through His Apostles, to the priests of today. The words of transubstantiation were first said by Jesus on Holy Thursday: *"Take and eat of it, take and drink of it."*

"Blessed are you, Lord God of all creation, for through your goodness we have received the bread we offer you; fruit of the earth and work of human hands. It will become for us the bread of life... Blessed are you, Lord God of all creation, for through your goodness we have received the wine we offer you; fruit of the vine and work of human hands. It will become our spiritual drink."

The words of the centurion, when begging Jesus to heal the centurion's servant, are repeated by Catholics before they receive the Eucharist. *"I am not worthy that you should enter under my roof, but only say the word and my soul will be healed."* These words, first uttered in Jesus' time and recorded in the Gospels, are repeated daily throughout the world in the context of the Mass. This demonstrates the awesome power of the Holy Mass.

A Brief Overview of My Typical Daily Prayer Routine

- Upon awakening I physically bless myself, *"In the name of the Father, and of the Son, and of the Holy Spirit. Amen."*
- Getting out of bed: I give thanks to the Father for a safe night's sleep and the opportunity to serve Him this new day.
- Opening window shades/blinds: I thank the Father for whatever type of day (sunny, rainy, snowy, etc.) and ask Him to bless my family, all religious, priests, friends, neighbors, fellow employees, our country, and the world. I pray for their physical, mental, and spiritual safety. (One to two minutes)
- I pray along with the daily televised rosary. (20 to 23 minutes)
- I listen to the homily from EWTN's daily televised Mass and recite the daily EWTN family prayer. (15 to 20 minutes)
- Before each meal: I pray with my spouse, family, or friends. *"Thank you, O Lord, for these Thy gifts which we are about to receive from Thy bounty, through Christ our Lord. Amen."* (10 seconds)
- After intimate marital relations: With my spouse, we privately offer a prayer of thanksgiving for the fruits and pleasures offered through the Sacrament of Marriage.
- When traveling to daily Mass: I recite the Chaplet of Divine Mercy with my wife. (7 to 8 minutes)

- I visit the exposition of the Blessed Sacrament before Holy Mass, offering prayers of thanksgiving and making special requests. (5 to 10 minutes)
- Before each Mass I talk to Jesus and the Blessed Mother, giving thanks for their suffering which made this Mass possible. (15 to 20 minutes)
- At Daily Mass: (see detailed description, pages 81-93) (45 minutes)
- Evening Prayers: (see detailed description, pages 74-79) (10 to 15 minutes)
- When going to bed, I physically bless myself and then review the day's activities. Just in case I die in my sleep, I say an Act of Contrition, which wipes away the venial sins I may have committed during the day. I end by thanking the Father for the opportunity to serve Him another day, and thank my guardian angel for his protection and guidance. (5 minutes)

Note: My daily prayer routine occasionally changes during days of travel or business commitments. When traveling, I always attempt to attend daily Mass.

My Additional Prayers and Activities

- I always carry rosary beads in my pocket. I occasionally hold them during business meetings and social events to keep the Blessed Mother and Holy Spirit close, allowing them to guide the group in activities that please the Father.

- Before attending a business meeting, I pray to the Holy Spirit to guide our decisions.
- During staff meetings at work, I recite an opening prayer, requesting guidance and understanding.
- At the close of each staff meeting, I recite a prayer of thanksgiving for a productive meeting.
- In large crowds such as at airports, movies, shows, Mass, and so on, I recite a quick prayer to the Holy Spirit, guardian angels, and Blessed Mother to protect and inspire all present, and keep them safe and in God's good graces.
- When flying, I recite a short prayer for everyone's safety before flying and a *"Thank you, Jesus"* upon landing.
- I keep a crucifix on the office wall, and periodically look at it while reciting, *"Thank you, Jesus, for suffering for us."*
- Every time an activity works out well, I silently thank God the Father, Jesus, and the Holy Spirit for the success.
- Periodically throughout the day, I offer a *"Thank you, Jesus, for my health and safety,"* and *"Thanks to the Father for this day, for the opportunity to serve Him."*
- Whenever I see a person with a physical problem, I say a short prayer: *"Help them, Jesus,"* or *"Have mercy on them, Jesus."*
- When watching a good performance by a singer, musician, actor, or athlete, I thank God for giving them their talent which allows me to

enjoy wholesome entertainment that is pleasing to God.
- I recite prayers of thanksgiving for good news and prayers of forgiveness for bad news.
- When seeing an accident reported on television news, I recite a short *"Help them, Jesus,"* for the injured and first responders.
- I pray for people with addictions and disorders, saying, *"Help them, Jesus."*
- I pray for people engaged in evil activities. *"Forgive them, Jesus; they know not what they are doing."*
- I pray for politicians who use God's name in vain to promote their political image, including those that say, *"God Bless America,"* while actively working to take away or restrict religious freedom. For these I pray, *"Forgive them, Father, for they do not know what they are doing."*
- Before going to sleep, I listen to the audio Bible or EWTN radio programs.
- If I wake up in the middle of the night, I thank God for this night and try to listen to what He, Jesus, the Holy Spirit, or the Blessed Mother may be trying to tell me.
- If I can't get back to sleep, at times I listen to the audio Bible, paying attention to what the Holy Spirit may be saying to me through the Scriptures. At other times I pray the rosary.
- Each day I try to sit quietly alone in my prayer room, surrounded by a crucifix, holy pictures, religious statues, and the Stations of the Cross. I call upon the Holy Spirit, *"Come, Holy Spirit, come,"* to help me understand God's will for me.

- When passing a cemetery, I recite one of the following short prayers: *"My Jesus, have mercy on them,"* or *"May they all rest in peace,"* or *"Eternal rest grant unto them all, Lord, and let perpetual light shine upon them. May their souls and all the souls of the faithful departed through the mercy of God rest in peace. Amen."*
- I also recite a daily prayer from the book *Every Day Is a Gift* by the Catholic Book Publishing Company in New York. In this book is prayer for each day of the year that is taken from the Gospels, with a reflection by a saint or the Holy Father.

Prayer Spaces I Have Created

Home: I place a crucifix or religious symbol in every room. Outside the house I have statues of Jesus and the Blessed Mother to show that a family that loves Jesus lives within. In my bedroom, I placed a crucifix over the bed, and keep a small crucifix under the mattress (an old family tradition), and a rosary and prayer books on the night table. While sleeping I keep a rosary around my arm or in my hand.

My prayer room: I created a special prayer room that contains a crucifix, the Stations of the Cross, and religious statues of the Blessed Mother and the risen Christ. In this room I have a special place for prayer and contemplation, where I also engage in Bible study, and read about or watch programs about the lives of the saints. This room also has a treadmill where I exercise while praying, and a television for watching religious programs. I recommend placing a crucifix over or near every television or computer in the house.

In my car: I keep a rosary in the door compartment and a crucifix and religious symbol on the dashboard.

In my office at work: I have a crucifix on the wall, a rosary on my desk, and pictures of my family and religious people (the pope, Jesus, the Blessed Mother, and Mother Angelica) in my office.

On my person: I wear religious medals and a scapular, and carry a religious card in my wallet which reads, *"If injured in an accident call a priest."* I carry a rosary in my pocket which I hold or touch when in danger or encountering anything of a serious nature.

Details of My Daily Prayers

Note: My actual words are *italicized*.

Upon Awakening:
- I bless myself and say: *"Thank You, Father, for giving me this good sleep and for allowing me to serve You this day."*
- Upon opening the window shades to look out on the weather, I say: *"Thank You, Father, for this weather and for the opportunity to serve You with the help of the Holy Spirit and my guardian angel. I ask for Your blessings for all my friends and family, for priests and religious, especially for _____ during their time of difficulty. I also ask for Your mercy for all the suffering people of this world, those suffering physically, mentally,*

A Journey to Holiness

and spiritually, especially for _____. Please also give Your mercy to all the souls in Purgatory. Ease their pain of being away from You. Give them peace and, if at all possible, please have the Blessed Mother, St. Joseph, St. Anne, St. Joachim, with St. Joseph's mom and dad, and our Heavenly family visit with all your future saints to give them a brief time of respite from their suffering."

- "Father, you know what is in my heart for solving the problems of the world. You know so much more of what needs to be done to make this world as You intended. Please let Your will be done, even if it may appear to bring pain and suffering to me and my family, my friends, my church, and my country."
- "Father, I trust You and again thank You for allowing Your Son Jesus and His mother to suffer so very much for us and our world. I shall be eternally grateful to Your Son for opening the gates of Heaven and showing us the way to please You."
- After getting a glass of juice or coffee, I recite, *"Bless us, O Lord, for these Thy gifts............"*
- Usually, while on the treadmill, I will recite the rosary. I personally end each decade of the rosary with: *"Jesus, Mary, and Joseph, save souls,"* or *"My Jesus, mercy; O Mary, conceived without sin, pray for us who have recourse to thee."*

During the Day:
- I attend daily Mass at my local parish, local shrine, monastery, or the chapel at work (see prayers recited during Mass, page 81).
- In the early evening after supper, I go into my prayer room, close the door and quietly recite

the following prayers. (I have modified many of the following generic prayers and those which have been taken from the *Catholic Book of Prayers*, edited by the Rev. Maurus Fitzgerald, O.F.M., Catholic Book Publishing Company, New York.)

"Remember, O most gracious Virgin Mary, that never was it known, that anyone who fled to thy protection, implored thy help, or sought thy intercession, was left unaided. Inspired with this confidence, I fly unto thee, O virgin of virgins my mother; to thee do I come, before thee I stand, sinful and sorrowful; O Mother of the Word Incarnate, despise not my petitions, but in thy clemency hear and answer me. Amen." (The Memorare)

"O Blessed Mother, please intercede to your son Jesus and to God the Father for the physical and spiritual strength, good health, and well-being of all who work for the Church in any way, so they may bring many souls to you. For the Holy Father, cardinals, bishops, priests, brothers, monks, nuns, and all the lay people—for everyone performing even the smallest service for the Church."

I pray to St. Anne and St. Joachim, to thank them for their protection and assistance for my health and safety, and especially for all the times they helped me with my physical and health issues. I ask them to help all of my family, friends, and religious, the same way they have helped me become closer to their daughter, Mary, and their grandson, Jesus.

"St. Anne and St. Joachim, please continue to protect me physically and spiritually and help all my friends and families in their time of need. Help them as you have helped me.

"But as always, let the Father's will be done, as He knows what is best for me."

Praying to God, the Source of Health

"God our Father, source of all health, be near those who suffer in times of weakness and pain, relieve them of their burdens and heal them, if it be Your will. Give peaceful sleep to those who need rest for the soul and body and be with them in their hours of silence. Bless those who do not know what another day will bring. Make them ready for whatever it may be. Whether they must stand, sit, or be confined, grant them a strong spirit. Inspire with Your love those who bring healing and care to the suffering. May they bestow Your gifts of health and strength wherever they go. Grant this prayer through Christ our Lord. Amen."

Praying for the Dead:

"God our Father, Your power brings us to birth, Your Providence guides our lives, and by Your command we are returned to dust.

"I pray for the dead, especially for (family, friends, religious, etc.). May all those who have been dear to me in life find a place with You in Heaven.

"Lord, those who die still live in Your presence; their lives have changed but did not end. I pray in hope for my family, relatives, and friends, and for all the dead known to You alone.

"In company with Christ who died and now lives, may they rejoice in Your kingdom where all our tears are wiped away. Unite us together again as one family to sing Your praises for ever and ever."

Praying for My Departed Relatives, Friends, and Benefactors:

"Heavenly Father, accept my prayer for all those in Purgatory for whom I should pray because of ties of family, gratitude, justice, or charity. Have mercy on my relatives, friends, and benefactors as well as those who hold positions of authority, both civil and religious. Admit them all to Your eternal happiness in Heaven. Eternal rest grant to them, Lord. And let perpetual light shine upon them. May they all rest in peace."

Praying for All the Faithful Departed:

"Heavenly Father, I believe that in Your wisdom and justice You willed to purify all persons who die without having attained the state that they need for all eternity, all who have still to expiate completely the sins they committed on earth. I also believe that You have mercifully arranged that this process of purification can be aided by the prayers of the living, especially through the Holy Eucharist.

"Help me to pray for my brothers and sisters who departed from this world. May their time of purification be short and they be quickly guided into the holy light promised by our Lord to Abraham and his descendants. I offer You sacrifices and prayers of praise. Accept them for all the souls of the faithful departed and admit them all to Your Heavenly joy."

Prayer to My Guardian Angel:

"Angel of God, my guardian dear, to whom His love entrusts me here, ever this night be at my side, to light and guard, to rule and guide. Amen."

> Each person, when created by God, was given a guardian angel. Everyone should pray with their guardian angel, which personalizes their relationship."

"My faithful guardian angel, thank you for all your protection and guidance throughout the day, especially keeping me safe when working and driving. Stay close to me in my old age as I am not as thoughtful or observant as I was in my youth. Joe, I shall be grateful to you for all eternity and look forward to our friendship in Heaven. Thank you, Father, for assigning such a wonderful guardian to help me serve you and to protect me in this world."

Prayer to Jesus, Mary, and Joseph Before Going to Sleep:

"Jesus, Mary, and Joseph, I give you my heart and my soul. Jesus, Mary, and Joseph, assist me in my last agony. Jesus, Mary, and Joseph, may I sleep and rest in peace with you and with St. Anne and St. Joachim and my deceased wife, relatives, and friends."

My Prayer to Jesus:

"Jesus Christ, my God, I adore You and thank You for the many favors You have bestowed on me this day. I offer You my sleep and all the moments of this night, and I pray You preserve me from sin. Therefore, I place myself in Your Most Sacred Side and under the mantle of our Blessed Lady my Mother. May the holy Angels assist me and keep me in peace, and may Your blessing always be upon me."

My Prayer for the Safety of My Home:

"We beseech You, O Lord, to visit this home, and to drive far from it all the snares of the enemy. Let Your holy Angels dwell therein so as to preserve us in peace, and let Your blessings be always upon us. Through Christ our Lord, Amen."

My Prayer Before Going to Bed in the Evening:
"Oh my God, I am heartily sorry for ever having offended You, and I detest all my sins, because I dread the loss of Heaven and the pains of hell. But most of all, because they offend You, my God, who are all good and deserving of all my love. I firmly resolve with the help of Your grace, to confess my sins, to do penance, to amend my life, and avoid the near occasion of sin. Amen."

> "How wonderful each night, to be able to close my eyes to sleep, with the possibility of one day waking up to see Jesus in Heaven!"

Preparing for Daily and Sunday Mass

To be at your best when receiving Jesus and participating in the Holy Mass, you should prepare for daily and Sunday Mass. To do this, I generally read about the saint of the day and review the readings of the day, especially the Gospel, so that I will better understand God's word.

After entering the church and blessing myself with holy water, (blessing with holy water is a reenactment and reminder of our original baptism, and when used in faith cleanses us of venial sin) I then genuflect before entering the pew.

I then kneel down in the pew, thanking God the Father for the honor of allowing my presence in His house, as I give thanks for all His blessings for me and my family, friends, country, and the world. To prepare myself for Mass I arrive early to talk to God, saying,

"Here I am Lord, I come to do Your will," or "Speak, Lord, Your servant is listening." I then spend a few moments preparing myself for the Mass. Some churches offer a public rosary one half hour before Mass begins to help prepare your mind for the Mass. I participate if this is offered. Also, try to offer a prayer for the priest at Mass.

(See page 171 – "A Prayer for Our Pastor and Shepherd")

> When reciting the words of the Holy Mass, be sincere. Believe in every word you say. If you don't believe what you are saying, you will not be well disposed to receive the many graces offered at the Mass.

I usually take the time after Communion or at the end of Mass to offer additional prayers to thank God the Father, Jesus, and the Blessed Mother for allowing me to receive the Holy Eucharist at the Sacrifice of the Mass. I also use this time to listen to what God wants to tell me.

CCC 2729 The habitual difficulty in prayer is distraction. It can affect words and their meaning in vocal prayer; it can concern, more profoundly, him to whom we are praying, in vocal prayer (liturgical or personal), meditation and contemplative prayer. To set about hunting down distractions would be to fall into their trap, when all that is necessary is to turn back to our heart: for a distraction reveals to us what we are attached to, and this humble awareness before the Lord should awaken our preferential love for him and lead us resolutely to offer him our heart to be purified; therein lies the battle, the choice of which master to serve.

To avoid distractions and to help focus on the Mass, I generally keep my eyes closed and closely listen to God's words.

My Specific Private Prayers at Holy Mass

(My actual spoken or unspoken words are *italicized*.)

Note: The Holy Mass is made up of two major parts. First is the *Liturgy of the Word*, when we hear God's holy words in the readings and in the Gospel taken from the Bible, and the deacon or priest's homily. The second part is the *Liturgy of the Eucharist*, when we actually receive Jesus' body, blood, soul, and divinity in the Holy Eucharist.

The Holy Mass

Introductory Rites

Entrance Processional
[All stand]

> **Suggestion:** During the Entrance Procession, as the priest and ministers enter and pass my pew, I gently bow to the crucifix and priest to give them thanks for bringing us Jesus and His Holy Words.

Liturgical Greeting
[All together make the Sign of the Cross]
Priest: In the name of the Father, and of the Son, and of the Holy Spirit.
Congregation: *Amen.*
[The priest or another minister may then briefly introduce the Mass for that day, saying something about the readings, the feast, and/or the special occasion being celebrated.]

> **Suggestion:** Make it a practice to repeat the priest's words as he is saying them, quietly and to yourself. This will help you to focus and to remember them, helping to better understand and participate in the totality of the Mass.

Penitential Act

[The following is only one of the three optional Penitential Rites.]

Priest: Brethren (brothers and sisters), let us acknowledge our sins, and so prepare ourselves to celebrate the sacred mysteries.

Congregation: *I confess to almighty God*
and to you, my brothers and sisters
that I have greatly sinned,
in my thoughts and in my words,
in what I have done
and in what I have failed to do,
through my fault, through my fault,
through my most grievous fault;

Suggestion: With these words, humble yourself by striking your chest three times.

Therefore, I ask blessed Mary ever-Virgin, all the Angels and Saints,
and you, my brothers and sisters,
to pray for me to the Lord our God.

Priest: May almighty God have mercy on us, forgive us our sins, and bring us to everlasting life.

Congregation: *Amen.*

Kyrie

Priest: Lord, have mercy.
Congregation: *Lord, have mercy.*
Priest: Christ, have mercy.
Congregation: *Christ, have mercy.*
Priest: Lord, have mercy.
Congregation: *Lord, have mercy.*

Priest: May almighty God cleanse us of our sins, and through the celebration of this Eucharist make us worthy to share at the table of His Kingdom.
Congregation: *Amen.*

Gloria

Congregation: *Glory to God in the highest, and on earth peace to people of good will. We praise You, we bless You, we adore You, we glorify You, we give You thanks for Your great glory. Lord God, heavenly King, O God, almighty Father. Lord Jesus Christ, Only Begotten Son, Lord God, Lamb of God, Son of the Father. You take away the sins of the world, have mercy on us; You take away the sins of the world, receive our prayer; You are seated at the right hand of the Father, have mercy on us. For You alone are the Holy One, You alone are the Lord. You alone are the Most High, Jesus Christ, with the Holy Spirit, in the glory of God the Father. Amen.*

Priest: Let us pray.
Congregation: *Amen.*
[All sit]

Liturgy of the Word

> **Suggestion:** Keep your eyes closed to better understand God's words and to avoid distractions.

First Reading

Lector: A reading from the Book of... [*or* the Letter of..., *or* the Acts of the Apostles]
Lector: The Word of the Lord.
Congregation: *Thanks be to God!*

Responsorial Psalm

[The choir and/or cantor sings or recites the psalm; the congregation joins in for the repeated response.]

Second Reading

[A second reading is prescribed for all Sundays and major feasts, but is omitted for most weekdays or minor feasts]

[All stand]

Alleluia or Gospel Acclamation

Choir or Cantor: Alleluia!
Congregation: *Alleluia!*
Choir or Cantor: *[verse]*
Congregation: *Alleluia!*

Note: During Lent the Alleluia is replaced with "Praise to you, Lord Jesus Christ, King of endless glory."

Gospel

> **Suggestion:** Keep your eyes closed to avoid distractions and pay attention to God's word.

Before the Gospel Proclamation:
Deacon (or Priest): The Lord be with you.
Congregation: *And with your spirit.* Deacon (or Priest): A reading from the Holy Gospel according to... *[Matthew, Mark, Luke, or John]*
Congregation: *Glory to you, O Lord!*

After the Gospel Proclamation:
Deacon (or Priest): The Gospel of the Lord.
Congregation: *Praise to you, Lord Jesus Christ!*

[All sit]

Homily: The priest or deacon offers a sermon on the readings or on a topic that brings the faith alive for the faithful.

[All stand]

Profession of Faith

The congregation recites the Universal Prayer (a.k.a. Prayer of the Faithful, or Bidding Prayers)

Lector: ...Let us pray to the Lord.

Congregation: *Lord, hear our prayer (or a similar response, repeated after each petition).*

[All sit]

Liturgy of the Eucharist

Presentation and Preparation of the Gifts

> **Suggestion:** Repeat the priest's words silently to absorb the meaning of the preparation of the gifts.

Priest: Blessed are you, Lord God of all creation, for through Your goodness we have received the bread we offer You: fruit of the earth and work of human hands, it will become for us the bread of life.

Congregation: *Blessed be God forever.*

Priest: Blessed are You, Lord God of all creation, for through Your goodness we have received the wine we offer you: fruit of the vine and work of human hands, it will become our spiritual drink.

Congregation: *Blessed be God forever.*

> **Suggestion:** During the Offertory of Mass, when the priest is offering the bread and wine, take any problems or sufferings that you may be experiencing, along with the sufferings of others, and offer them along with the consecration of the bread and wine.

> Later in the Mass when the priest says, "THIS IS MY BODY," and "THIS IS MY BLOOD," offer your sufferings up with the bread and wine, and trust that Christ will not only transform the bread and wine into His body and blood, but He will also take your sufferings and join them to His own, accepting them as a sacrifice from you to the Father.

[All stand]

Then, after the priest has washed his hands and the music is finished, he invites the people to join in prayer:

Priest: Pray, brethren (brothers and sisters), that my sacrifice and yours may be acceptable to God, the almighty Father.

Congregation: *May the Lord accept the sacrifice at your hands, for the praise and glory of His name, for our good, and the good of all His Holy Church.*

Prayer Over the Offerings

[The priest sings or says this prayer, which is different for each Mass. At the end, the people sing or say in response:]

Congregation: *Amen.*

Eucharistic Prayers

Note: The posture of the people during the Eucharistic Prayer is different in various countries and regions; in the United States, the people normally stand until the "*Sanctus*," and then kneel until the concluding "Amen" has been said.

Preface Dialogue

Priest: The Lord be with you.
Congregation: *And with your spirit.*
Priest: Lift up your hearts.
Congregation: *We lift them up to the Lord.*
Priest: Let us give thanks to the Lord, our God.
Congregation: *It is right and just.*

Sanctus

Congregation: *Holy, holy, holy, Lord God of hosts,*
Heaven and earth are full of Your glory.
Hosanna in the highest.
Blessed is He who comes in the name of the Lord.
Hosanna in the highest.
[All kneel]

The Eucharistic Prayer

Priest: On the day before He was to suffer, He took bread in His holy and venerable hands, and with eyes raised to Heaven to You, O God, His almighty Father, giving You thanks, He said the blessing, broke the bread and gave it to His disciples, saying:

[When the priest is elevating the Host, he prays facing the people saying:]

"TAKE THIS, ALL OF YOU, AND EAT OF IT, FOR THIS IS MY BODY, WHICH WILL BE GIVEN UP FOR YOU."

(My personal words) As I look upon the Holy Eucharist, I pray: *"My Lord and My God. Forgive me, Jesus, for I am a sinner and do not deserve you."*

Priest: In a similar way, when supper was ended, He took this precious chalice in His holy and venerable hands, and once more giving you thanks, He said the blessing and gave the chalice to His disciples, saying:

[As the priest is elevating the cup, he prays facing the people:]

"TAKE THIS, ALL OF YOU, AND DRINK FROM IT, FOR THIS IS THE CHALICE OF MY BLOOD, THE BLOOD OF THE NEW AND ETERNAL COVENANT, WHICH WILL BE POURED OUT FOR YOU AND FOR MANY FOR THE FORGIVENESS OF SINS. DO THIS IN MEMORY OF ME."

(My personal words) As I look upon the Eucharistic cup of Jesus' blood, I pray: *"Forgive me, Jesus, for all the times that I have received You unworthily, and cleanse me of my sins to make me worthy to receive You today and to faithfully serve You both here on earth and for all eternity in Heaven."*

Mystery of Faith (Memorial Acclamation)

Priest: The mystery of faith:

Congregation: [Version A] *"We proclaim your death, O Lord, and profess Your Resurrection until You come again."*

[or B] *"When we eat this Bread and drink this Cup, we proclaim Your death, O Lord, until You come again."*

[or C] *"Save us, Savior of the world, for by Your Cross and Resurrection, You have set us free."*

Doxology and Great Amen
Priest: Through Him, and with Him, and in Him, O God, almighty Father, in the unity of the Holy Spirit, all glory and honor is Yours, for ever and ever.
Congregation: *Amen!*
[May be sung more than once]

Communion Rite
[All stand]

The Lord's Prayer

> **Suggestion:** Keep your eyes closed and try to visualize Jesus teaching the disciples how to pray the Our Father.

Priest: At the Savior's command and formed by divine teaching, we dare to say:
Congregation: *Our Father, who art in Heaven, hallowed be Thy name;*
Thy kingdom come; Thy will be done on earth as it is in Heaven
Give us this day our daily bread;
and forgive us our trespasses as we forgive those who trespass against us;
and lead us not into temptation, but deliver us from evil.
Priest: Deliver us, Lord, we pray, from every evil, and graciously grant peace in our days, that, by the help of Your mercy, we may be always free from sin

and safe from all distress, as we await the blessed hope and the coming of our Savior, Jesus Christ.

Congregation: *For the kingdom, the power, and the glory are Yours, now and forever.*

The Sign of Peace

Priest: Lord Jesus Christ, who said to your Apostles, Peace I leave you, my peace I give you, look not on our sins, but on the faith of your Church, and graciously grant her peace and unity in accordance with your will. Who live and reign for ever and ever.

Congregation: *Amen.*

Priest: The peace of the Lord be with you always.

Congregation: *And with your spirit.*

Deacon or Priest: Let us offer each other a sign of peace.

[The ministers and all the people exchange an embrace, handshake, or other appropriate gesture of peace with those near them, according to local custom.]

Fraction of the Bread (The Host)

[We know the host to be the body, blood, soul, and divinity of Jesus Christ. It's what sets us apart from all other religions.]

Congregation: *Lamb of God, You take away the sins of the world: have mercy on us.*

Lamb of God, You take away the sins of the world: have mercy on us.

Lamb of God, You take away the sins of the world: grant us peace.

[All kneel]

[The "Lamb of God" may be sung or recited, and may be repeated several more times until the breaking of bread and the preparation of the communion vessels are finished; but the last phrase is always "Grant us peace."]

Communion
Priest: Behold the Lamb of God, behold Him who takes away the sins of the world. Blessed are those called to the supper of the Lamb.
Congregation: *Lord, I am not worthy that You should enter under my roof, but only say the word and my soul shall be healed.*

> **Suggestion:** Try to pray the Act of Contrition before receiving Communion, to help assure that you are free of any venial sins committed during Mass, even after reciting the penitential rite prayer at the beginning of the Mass.

The Act of Contrition: *"O my God, I am heartily sorry for ever having offended Thee and I detest all my sins, because I dread the loss of Heaven and the pains of hell, but most of all because they offend You, my God, who are all good and deserving of all my love. I firmly resolve, with the help of Your grace, to confess my sins, to do penance, and to amend my life. Amen."*

> **While not required, I add the following:** *"...and to sin no more and to avoid the near occasion of sin and to please forgive me for all the times I may have received Jesus unworthily! Amen."*

"A soul can do nothing more pleasing than to receive communion in a state of grace." St. Alphonsus Liguori

Note: A soul commits a sacrilege (the most serious offense against God) by receiving Communion in a state of mortal sin.

> **Suggestion:** Genuflect before receiving the body and the blood of Christ, always saying, *"My Jesus, have mercy on me, a sinner."*

Eucharistic Minister: The Body of Christ.
Communicant: *Amen.*
Communion Minister: The Blood of Christ.
Communicant: *Amen.*

Communion Song

During the reception of Communion, an appropriate song is sung, or a short "Communion Antiphon" is recited.

[All sit]

Period of Silence *or* **Song of Praise:**

Note: When we receive Jesus in the Holy Eucharist, we experience no greater intimacy with God on earth.

The following is only one of many examples of the power of the Holy Eucharist!

There is magnificent power in receiving the Holy Eucharist in a state of grace.

Blessed Alexandrina Maria da Costa did not eat food or drink water for thirteen years. She survived solely on the sustenance she received in daily Communion from 1942 to 1955.

This example is one of the many ways in which Jesus has shown the world the power of the Eucharist and the power He has over souls.

Blessed Alexandrina Maria da Costa of Balasar, Portugal, (1904–1955) one of the great mystics of modern times, was beatified by Pope John Paul II in 2004. A "victim soul," chosen by Christ to suffer in atonement for the sins of humanity, she was bedridden from the age of twenty after sustaining injuries while escaping from an attacker. She mystically shared in Christ's Passion on Fridays. Her sufferings are credited with helping shorten World War II. Her astounding life has many connections to the events of Fatima, and she is known in Portugal as the *"fourth seer of Fatima."*

Blessed Alexandrina said on her deathbed to those in her room and to the world, *"Do not sin. The pleasures of this life are worth nothing. Receive Communion. Pray the Rosary every day. This sums up everything."*

"Do penance, sin no more, pray the Rosary, receive the Eucharist." For the last thirteen years of her life, Alexandrina miraculously lived on the Holy Eucharist alone; a medically confirmed fact. She has been proposed by the Church as "a model of purity and perseverance in the Faith for today's youth."

> **Suggestion:** Right after receiving Communion and returning to the pew, kneel down and give thanks to Jesus and His mother for all that they suffered to make the Mass possible. Then thank God for all His love and blessings.

This is when I pray to Jesus and the Holy Spirit for my family, friends, those who are suffering, and the souls in Purgatory. I say special prayers to the Blessed Mother for priests, deacons, religious, and anyone who works for the Church in any way. This includes all those employed by EWTN, and the benefactors and viewers. I also have a special prayer for Mother Mary Angelica and the nuns of her order. I pray for our country and all sinners. I give thanks for my deceased relatives and friends.

I pray for God's mercy for all the unworthy Communions that are taken daily throughout the world, including the times that I have received when I may have not been totally worthy.

I call for the Holy Spirit to come to us here in the congregation, and bring us closer to the Father through the reception of the Holy Eucharist. Finally, I ask Him to bless the people who did not receive the Eucharist today.

Prayer after Communion

Priest: Let us pray.

[The congregation prays in silence, unless a period of silence has already been observed. Then the priest sings or says the Prayer after Communion, which is different for each Mass. At the end, the people proclaim their consent.]

Congregation: *Amen.*

Concluding Rites

[Announcements, etc.]

[If there are any announcements, remembrances, acknowledgements, reflections, or similar actions, they are required to be spoken here. The people may remain standing, or may be invited to sit, depending on the length of the announcements or other activity.]

[All Stand]

Final Blessing

Dismissal

Deacon (or Priest): Go forth, the Mass is ended.
[or] Go and announce the Gospel of the Lord.
[or] Go in peace, glorifying the Lord by your life.
[or] Go in peace.
Congregation: *Thanks be to God!*

[Recessional/Closing Song]

[It is traditional in many countries and parishes to sing a final song or have some instrumental music played as the priest and ministers process out of the church. However, this is optional as it is not prescribed in the Order of Mass.]

> **Suggestion:** As the priest and ministers process off the altar and pass by my pew, I gently bow to the crucifix and give quiet thanks to the priest, who brought me Jesus in the Eucharist and God's Holy Word.

"On that day you will know that I am in my Father and you are in me, and I in you." (John 14:20)

> After Mass, plan to spend a few extra minutes on your knees to give thanks for the sacrifice of the Mass. Jesus remains physically within us for approximately fifteen to twenty minutes after we receive Him into our bodies in the Eucharist.

Praying During Dark Days and Difficult Times

Everyone at some time in their life experiences dark days and difficult times during which prayer is difficult. Getting through these times will make you stronger in your faith. Always remember that God loves you and will never allow you a cross or a difficulty that is more than you can manage.

A quote that has been attribute to Blessed Mother Teresa of Calcutta goes like this: *"I know, Lord, that you don't give anyone more than they can handle, but sometimes I think you may have mistaken me for someone else."*

Know that God will always love you, no matter what road you take in life. Many of our greatest saints have gone through dark days: St. Augustine, St. Therese, St. Padre Pio, St. Francis, and Mother Teresa. You should know that you are not the first to experience the dark days and the temptations of the devil. If it happened to the saints, there's no reason it can't happen to you.

> Personally, I have never met any adult who has not experienced dark days or difficult times during their life.

During dark days your attitude on every issue can be negative. You are not happy. Satan will take advantage of your depression and negative thoughts. This will become evident in your behavior and conversations. Everyone at some time experiences the absence of a desire to pray. At this time your reasoning is clouded with doubt and confusion about how much God really loves you.

I experienced my darkest days when my holy, loving wife, was called by God unexpectedly after forty-two years of marriage. Those dark days did not start immediately. Several weeks after her death, while making pilgrimages to shrines, Satan took advantage of my dark days. It was awful and intense—like nothing else I had ever experienced. Not only did I experience doubts about everything I knew, I also had doubts about my family, my faith, and my prayer life. Worse yet, I had serious sexual thoughts and fantasies about extreme actions, including drinking and drugs. This was not me. Satan was hard at work, throwing all kinds of doubts and desires at me to turn me away from God, and stop my journeys to the shrines. My only defense was prayer. I couldn't understand why this was happening to me. When I confessed this to a priest on my travels in Canada, he urged me not to leave the Church or the sacraments.

Yes, those were very serious, dark days! I was ready to give up all the good I had worked for in my life—up to and including my salvation in Heaven. I fought against these negative thoughts, doubts, and decisions with constant prayer. While this was happening, I tried all the harder to turn back to God.

One day, while traveling in my car, I stopped at three different Catholic churches on my way to shrines in Canada. I prayed the rosary and made the Stations of the Cross. I wanted to spend time in God's house, away from the temptations Satan was throwing at me. I just didn't understand why I had such a strong desire to experience evil. Hindsight is always twenty-twenty. But occasionally everyone, especially those who are close to God, will be attacked by Satan, who casts doubt on our faith. God may allow these tests, **but never more than we can handle.**

"No trial has come to you but what is human. God is faithful and will not let you be tried beyond your strength: but with the trial He will also provide a way out, so that you may be able to bear it." (1 Corinthians 10:13)

Our Church provides us with the resources to defend ourselves during dark times: prayer, the rosary, the Chaplet of Divine Mercy, the Stations of the Cross, the Bible, and the Sacraments of Confession and Holy Communion. We also have the crucifix, holy medals, and scapulars that we wear and carry, which brings us protection from our Blessed Mother and guardian angels. After the passing of my wife, I carried a crucifix in my pocket for months, and when temptations came I held the crucifix in my hand!

> When we are faced with making any serious decision, we should always first pray for the guidance to make the right decision. Right decisions bring us closer to God; the wrong ones lead us away from Him. The popular acronym W.W.J.D. (What Would Jesus Do?) should always preface every major decision.

Changes in our physical and mental condition happen all the time. Sometimes these changes can be drastic, at which time you can become more vulnerable to stress, confusion, indecision, etc. Be careful when taking medication or drinking alcohol during these times, as they can often cause mental confusion and have serious side effects that can affect your spiritual life.

A Prayer to Jesus When Taking Strong Medications

(Given to me by a nurse friend who takes and has dispensed medications.)

"Jesus, You are the Divine Physician and we know that all healing comes through You. Thank You for the gift of medication, which You can use for healing my body. Please block any adverse reactions or side effects from this drug which my doctor has advised me to take, and let it be a source of Your healing power. Holy Spirit, please give me the wisdom and understanding to hear Your voice and grant me peace in knowing You are in charge of all things which pertain to my life."

> When you are in a weakened position you are most vulnerable to Satan's power. His influence is deceptive, providing a path which appears to be in our best interest, and at the same time, pleasing to God. Don't be fooled by him! You are in a fight with Satan to save your eternal soul. You must use the armor and weapons God and our Church have given us to combat sin and evil in its many forms. Prayers including the rosary and Chaplet of Divine Mercy, the Holy Mass, the sacraments, having a spiritual advisor—these are all powerful weapons that will protect us.

The Catholic Church has been described as a hospital for sinners. Jesus was asked why He ate with tax collectors and sinners. He answered them, *"Those who are well have no need of the physician, but the sick do; I came not to call the righteous, but sinners."* (Mark 2:17)

Don't put yourself into an occasion of sin. For example, a person who has a drinking problem should not hang out in a bar. Even one drink can weaken the ability to control a desire for alcohol. Someone susceptible to immoral sex should avoid movies or internet programming that promotes illicit sex.

In our Catholic life we take certain vows before God. These include renewing our baptismal vows (every year at Easter), receiving Holy Communion and Confirmation, and our marriage vows. These are the most powerful serious obligations that we, as laypeople, will ever enter into. No legal contract is greater than the spiritual contract we make with God in our holy vows, which are spiritually binding in Heaven and to which we will be held accountable.

God loves every person He created equally, just as parents love their children equally. Regardless of how each person decides to live his or her life, or how far the soul turns away from God, He will always love them as much as the soul who has been faithful to Him.

Our Dark Days Bring Us Closer to God

I sincerely believe that God allows difficult times throughout our lives so that we can prove to Him, through our free will, how much we really love Him. In spite of our dark days, we choose to follow Him and keep His commandments.

The Bible recounts a time when God tested man's love. God asked Abraham to sacrifice his son, and without hesitation, Abraham took his son to the mountain to fulfill God's command. Abraham proved his love, and God rewarded him by promising that his descendants would be as numerous as the stars. God also promised our salvation because of Abraham's love and obedience. **Thank you, Father Abraham!**

> "Do not allow yourselves to be overly sad by the unfortunate accidents of the world. You are not aware of the benefits that they bring and by what secret judgment of God they are arranged for the eternal joy of the elect." St. John of the Cross

"We know that all things work for good for those who love God, who are called according to his purpose." (Romans 8:28)

Why Does God Permit Evil In His Creation?

The short classic answer by learned scholars like St. Augustine and St. Thomas:

"God permits evil so as to bring about a greater good."

> CCC 324 The fact that God permits physical and even moral evil is a mystery that God illuminates by his Son Jesus Christ who died and rose to vanquish evil. Faith gives us the certainty that God would not permit an evil if he did not cause a good to come from that very evil, by ways that we shall fully know only in eternal life.

> "When you listen to God and you do it His way, you will have holiness, health, and happiness. If you disobey Him, you will be in trouble." Cardinal Timothy Dolan

CHAPTER 4

Inspirations and Beliefs

"To the greater glory of God."
St. Ignatius of Loyola

> In this chapter I share my Catholic inspirations and beliefs and describe how they have affected my prayer life. These inspirations were acquired over the past eighty years from many Catholic sources including the Bible, the Catechism of the Catholic Church, homilies at Mass, instructional religious programs, and generational religious beliefs and practices.

Life and Suffering

"[There is a] time to give birth, and a time to die." (Ecclesiastes 3:2)

We were born and we will die; we will also have difficult experiences throughout our lives that will affect our prayer life. Look forward to and plan how you will manage your suffering. Offer it back to Jesus and Mary for their suffering on our behalf. **Think of suffering as a form of love.**

> Who suffered more in the history of the world than Jesus and His mother Mary? Why? Was it not because of their love for God and for us?

You might also try to imagine how much God the Father really loves us, to have allowed His Son and the Blessed Mother, who He greatly loves, to suffer so much for our benefit. **What greater love is possible?**

Our Eternal Soul

There is no death to our eternal soul. When we were created by God, our soul was placed simultaneously into our body. We will pass through four phases during our existence. The first phase took place in our mother's womb. The second phase started when we were born into the present world. The third phase when we die and pass into eternity. And the fourth and final phase takes place when we receive our bodies back at the General Resurrection. We will have a human body during all the phases of our existence—even after resurrection day. On that day our human body will be reunited with our soul.

Our physical body will cease to function when we die, but our soul continues to exist. We should never fear leaving this phase and moving into the next. In fact, we should look forward to the final stages of our earthly life. If we could ask a baby in the womb if it wants to be born, I'm sure it would respond that it was perfectly comfortable and would rather not go through the stress of birth. When we think about passing into the next world, we feel the same way—comfortable in this present life. Perhaps God allows more pain and suffering as we get older so that we can look forward to "passing on" to our next life, where there will be no pain and suffering.

God's Love for Us

God created us out of love. Do you ever think you are unworthy of God's love?
- Have you ever persecuted Jesus and His followers? St. Paul did.
- Have you lived with a woman out of wedlock for seventeen years and fathered an illegitimate child? St. Augustine did.
- Have you performed thousands of abortions? A leader of the pro-life movement once did.
- Have you denied Jesus three times? St. Peter did.

> Join the world of sinners and serve God. You, too, can become a saint!

Some of the greatest saints of the Catholic Church were sinners. Some of them were infamous sinners: St. Paul, St. Augustine, King David, to name just a few. We are all sinners, but we are all loved by God unconditionally and He will never stop or reduce His love for us.

The Extent to Which God Loves Us

We are the stewards of our bodies and souls, which God created out of His love for us.

> Regardless of how bad or neglectful we are, God's love is always with us. Of course, just as children disappoint their parents, we can disappoint our Father. God is not disappointed because our sinful actions hurt Him, but rather, because they hurt us.

What kind of parent loves one child more than another? Doesn't every parent want the best for his or her children? **We must remember that God is all love, but, He is also all just in His judgments of His children.**

God's Will for Us

Lord, what do you will for me? What is my destiny? *"He destined us in love to be his sons through Jesus Christ, according to the purpose of his will, to the praise of his glorious grace, which he freely bestows on us in the Beloved."* (Ephesians 1:5-6)

> *CCC 2826 By prayer we can discern "what is the will of God" and obtain the endurance to do it.* ***Jesus teaches us that one enters the kingdom of Heaven not by speaking words, but by doing "the will of my Father in Heaven."***

God freely gives us His grace, as needed, to help us carry out His will for our destiny—to be with Him for all eternity. God's plan for us is to be and do good! God does not plan for us to sin. Because He gave us free will, we choose to sin.

God gave us wisdom and insight to help us understand His will. Insight is the ability to comprehend. Wisdom is practical knowledge.

"What good is it for you to give God one thing when He asks for something else? Discover what God wants and do it. Your heart will be happier than if your own desire had been fulfilled." St. John of the Cross

St. Ignatius of Loyola gave the Jesuits a motto: *"To the greater glory of God."* This is the purpose and destiny of each human being. When we make decisions we should always ask ourselves how this decision can help to bring greater glory to God. Is our decision for the greater glory of God, or is it for my personal glory? While many decisions will be made for good reasons, will they ultimately be for the greater glory of God?

God Gives Us Examples of How We Can Please Him

Throughout history God has chosen unlikely people to influence and teach His people. St. Peter and the Apostles, who were simple uneducated fishermen and tentmakers, and the children of Fatima, and St. Bernadette of Lourdes, are just a few examples. He chooses simple people to show us that the grace of God enables common people to accomplish great things. This is a powerful way in which He spreads His word.

In our own time God called upon Mother Mary Angelica, a Poor Clare nun, to bring God's word to millions of people around the world, increasing their devotion to God. She did this by starting a world-wide religious media network, the Eternal World Television Network (EWTN) which includes radio and television stations, and a newspaper, the National Catholic Register. In spite of all the odds against her (having only $200 when beginning these endeavors) and the many obstacles that were in her way, God worked through her to accomplish what many considered to be impossible.

> Blessed Fulton Sheen said, *"To swim against the current of the culture and do what is right takes the strong. Dead bodies float with the current."*

As St. John Paul II once said about Mother Mary Angelica in his heavy Polish accent: *"Strong woman!"*

God Gives Us the Resources to Help Us on Our Journey to Heaven

God gave us the Ten Commandments through Moses. When His followers found the commandments difficult to follow, He sent His Son to show man how to serve and love one another. In the Sermon on the Mount, Jesus said, "I have not come to destroy the law but to fulfill it, to bring it to its greatest conclusion."

Jesus' life and teachings give us more examples of how to please God and to live a productive existence, and achieve everlasting life with Him in Heaven. To help us even more, He gave us the Mother of Jesus as an example, and to help us through her intercession with her Son. Remember, we must be like children, following the example of Jesus and Mary, trusting in God's laws, and refraining from interpreting His laws to fit the current culture.

The Communion of Saints

(Also known as:)
"I'LL PRAY FOR YOU—PLEASE PRAY FOR ME."

In Heaven, the saints can pray for us on earth and for the souls in purgatory.

They are the Church Triumphant.

(The souls that made it to Heaven)

In Purgatory, the souls (future saints) can only pray for us on earth through God, but not for themselves.

They are the Church Suffering.

(The souls that are being prepared for Heaven)

On earth, we humans can pray for the souls in purgatory.

We are the Church Militant.

(The souls that are striving for Heaven)

Together we are "The Communion of Saints." We are one family, pilgrims on earth. The souls in Purgatory are being cleansed** to become future saints in Heaven (the Church Triumphant). The faithful, who have reached their heavenly home, are now the saints in Heaven. Together we are ALL known as "The Communion of Saints" as we pray for one another. The prayers coming from the future saints in Purgatory (the Church Suffering) are especially powerful as they pray for us (the Church Militant) while they are suffering, separated from the beatific vision of God.

**"But nothing unclean will enter it (Heaven) nor anyone who does abominable things or tells lies." (Revelation 21:27)

> CCC 1475 In the communion of saints, "a perennial link of charity exists between the faithful who have already reached their heavenly home, those who are expiating their sins in purgatory and those who are still pilgrims on earth. Between them there is, too, an abundant exchange of all good things." In this wonderful exchange, the holiness of one profits others, well beyond the harm that the sin of one could cause others. Thus recourse to the communion of saints lets the contrite sinner be more promptly and efficaciously purified of the punishments for sin.

God's Laws

God gave Adam and Eve the first law which prohibited them from eating from the tree of knowledge. *"From that tree you shall not eat; when you eat from it you shall die."* (Genesis 2:17)

When they failed His ONLY COMMANDMENT, original sin came into the world. To help guide His followers and give them rules for living a God-pleasing life, God then gave Moses the Ten Commandments.

CCC 2067 "The Ten Commandments state what is required in the love of God and love of neighbor. The first three commandments concern love of God, and the other seven love of neighbor."

"'Teacher, what good deed must I do, to gain eternal life?'... 'If you wish to enter into eternal life, keep the commandments.'" (Matthew 19:16-17)

Jesus gave us the Beatitudes in the Sermon on the Mount to show us how to love. The Beatitudes are not laws, but guidelines on how to fulfill the Ten Commandments while living happily within the law. **(See pages 162-163)**

Offering Your Service to God

"Do not wait for old age to offer yourself to God. Offer Him the flower of your youth, which will be pleasing to Him and which He will accept with the greatest of love." St. Catherine of Siena

"Do not cast me aside in my old age; as my strength fails, do not forsake me." (Psalm 71:9)

Putting Self Before God

Our infinite longing is for God, but we tend to replace our desire to be with God with what St. Thomas Aquinas named the four classical substitutes: *wealth, pleasure, power, and honor,* which can be recognized in today's world as addictions that lead us away from God.

You Cannot Love God If You Are Thinking About Yourself!

You can only love God as much as you **are not** thinking about yourself! Satan wants us to constantly think about ourselves by excessively worrying about our health, aches and pains, financial problems, social status, reputation, and self-importance. When we are preoccupied with ourselves, when our focus is on us and our problems, we are not thinking about God or about how we can help others.

Leading therapists now recommend that their patients help others in need as a remedy for depression or other psychological problems. Helping others takes the mind off personal problems and puts problems in perspective.

> "If you want to be discouraged, keep looking into the mirror." **Cardinal Terence Cooke**

"**Thus,** the *last will be first, and the first will be last.*" *(Matthew 20:16)*

"*Amen, I say to you, whatever you did for one of these least brothers of mine, you did for me.*" *(Matthew 25:40)*

Love for God and Neighbor

When one of the Pharisees asked Jesus which commandment was the greatest, Jesus said to him, "*You shall love the Lord, your God, with your whole heart, with your whole soul, and with all your mind. This is the greatest and first commandment. The second is like it: You shall love your neighbor as yourself. On these two commandments the whole law is based.*" *(Matthew 22:37-40)*

How do we show or measure the amount of love that we have for God, who we cannot see, feel, or touch?

"*Blessed are those who have not seen and have believed.*" *(John 20:29)*

St. Paul, in his first letter to the Corinthians, told us, "*There are three things that last: faith, hope and love. But the greatest of these is love.*" *(13:13)* In Heaven, faith and hope will not exist; only love will remain.

God Talks to Us

"Therefore Eli said to Samuel, 'Go to sleep, and if He calls you shall say, "Speak, Lord, for your servant hears",' and when Samuel went to sleep and the Lord came, calling 'Samuel.' Samuel said 'Speak, for thy servant hears.'" (1 Samuel 3:9-10)

> St. Augustine said, "Your prayer is the word you speak to God. When you read the Bible, God speaks to you."

"Ignorance of Scripture is ignorance of Christ." St. Jerome

Thanking God for Marital Relations

Always offer thanks to the Father for all the pleasures of your marital relationship and for the gift that brings you and your spouse together.

"We must never fail to thank our Lord after we have received some sign of goodness, some benefit from Him. For God loves grateful hearts and heaps blessings on them." St. Mary Euphrasia

"Give thanks always and for everything in the name of our Lord Jesus Christ to God the Father." (Ephesians 5:20)

"Rejoice always, pray constantly, give thanks in all circumstances, for this is the will of God in Christ Jesus for you." (1 Thessalonians 5:16–18)

"A contrite and humbled heart, O God, you will not scorn." (Psalm 51:19)

Make God Part of Your Daily Life

Get into the habit of daily Scripture reading from the Bible or Catechism. St. Augustine said, *"Without God I can't; without me God won't."* God desires that we work with Him to bring ourselves closer to Him.

God's Plan for Us

"I therefore, a prisoner in the Lord, urge you to live in a manner worthy of the vocation in which you are called with all humility and mildness, with patience, supporting one another in love." (Ephesians 4:1) **This is the calling all of us have to serve one another.**

(See page 167 – "The Fourteen Works of Mercy")

When Jesus was speaking to the Apostles, He was also giving us instructions on how to work for Him and for His Father. He instructed Simon Peter to *"Feed my lambs…Tend my sheep…Feed my sheep."* (John 21:15-17)

Saint Padre Pio tells us, *"Prayer is the best weapon we have, a key that opens the heart of God. The door to your heart should be open to Him in holy confidence. Your body is not your own, it is the temple of the Holy Spirit."*

To know God's plan for us, Padre Pio recommends weekly confession, daily Communion, spiritual reading, meditation, and examination of conscience.

Giving Thanks

We must give constant thanks to God even for the things we don't like, since God is able to turn those things to our benefit. God doesn't like complainers, but He does understand our imperfect human nature.

"Give thanks in all circumstances; for this is the will of God in Christ Jesus for you." (1 Thessalonians 5:18)

"Ingratitude is the enemy of our immortal souls." St. Bernard

Giving God Thanks for Allowing Suffering

St. Brother Andre Bessette: At St. Joseph's Oratory in Montréal, Canada, thousands of believers came to Brother Andre seeking cures for their illnesses. **He would tell them to first thank God for their suffering because it was so valuable.** He also had them go to confession, if necessary. He would then pray with them. Most of the people he prayed with were cured. Brother Andre always refused credit for any of the healings. **He insisted that cures and healing were directly related to the person's faith in God, and through the intercession of St. Joseph.** St. Brother Andre had a great love for the Eucharist and is remembered for his deep devotion to St. Joseph, which helped him live a holy life. We can learn much from the examples of the saints. We can form close friendships with the saints by reading about their lives and praying for their intercession. They will show us how to live as good friends of Jesus, just as they did in life.

Jesus' Love for Us

> Blessed Mother Teresa of Calcutta once said, "When you look at the Crucifix, you understand how much Jesus loved you then. When you look at the Sacred Host you understand how much Jesus loves you now."

For Those of Faith: The Historical Evidence for the Real Presence of Jesus in the Eucharist

In 1263, a Bohemian priest known as Father Peter of Prague visited a church in Bolsena, Italy, to celebrate Mass. At the time, he was experiencing doubts about the real presence of Christ in the Eucharist. While Father Peter was serving Mass, just after he spoke the words of consecration, and elevated the sacred host, blood began to flow from the host, down his hands, and onto the corporal on the altar. Father Peter's faith was strengthened through that miracle. Today in the Cathedral in Orvieto, Italy, that same bloody Eucharist that Father Peter held is still on display above the altar, more than 750 years later! **It is totally uncorrupted.**

Being Lukewarm

"I know your works; I know that you are neither cold nor hot. I wish you were either cold or hot. So, because you are lukewarm, neither hot nor cold, I will vomit you out of my mouth." (Revelations 3:15-16)

St. Ambrose said, "The Word of God moves swiftly; He is not won by the lukewarm, nor held fast by the negligent. Let your soul be attentive to His word; follow carefully the path God tells you to take, for He is swift in His passing."

Faith and Suffering

"Through faith we understand that the universe was ordered by the Word of God, so that what is visible came into being by the invisible." (Hebrews 11:3)

"Understanding is the reward of faith, therefore seek not to understand that you may believe, but believe, that you may understand." St. Augustine

"Blessed are those who have not seen and have believed." (John 20:29)

St. Faustina wrote in her diary, "If the Angels were capable of envy they would envy us for two things. One, the ability to receive Holy Communion, and the other is the ability to suffer." Both put us into intimate spiritual contact with the Son of God.

St. Thérèse of Lisieux, the "Little Flower," wrote, "Everything is a grace; everything is the direct effect of our Father's love. Difficulties, contradictions, humiliations, are all the souls' miseries, burdens, needs. **Everything is a grace from the Father, including suffering.**"

Developing a Formal Prayer Life

"If you really want your love for Christ to grow and last then you must be faithful to prayer." St. John Paul II

If we are to be co-heirs with Jesus Christ in the Kingdom, then we must also share in His Passion and suffering as well.

CCC 2697 "We must remember God more often than we draw breath." But we cannot pray "at all times" if we don't pray at specific times, consciously willing it.

A good example which illustrates the meaning of this passage is the story of *Fiddler on the Roof*, a 1971 film which was based on the 1964 musical of the same name. Tevye, the father of the Jewish family depicted in this classic, makes it a practice to constantly talk to God. He engages in his weekly formal Jewish prayer with the rabbi, but also talks constantly to God throughout the day. God was certainly a major part of his life.

The Church Encourages Continual Prayer

CCC 2698 The Tradition of the Church proposes to the faithful certain rhythms of praying intended to nourish continual prayer. Some are daily, such as morning and evening prayer, grace before and after meals, the Liturgy of the Hours. Sundays, centered

on the Eucharist, are kept Holy primarily by prayer. The cycle of the liturgical year and its great feasts are also basic rhythms of the Christian's life of prayer.

"The most powerful prayer is silent adoration before the Blessed Sacrament." St. John Paul II

"Let nothing disturb you, let nothing trouble you, everything passes, God alone remains. God never changes. Patience achieves everything. Whoever has God lacks nothing." St. Teresa of Avila

Preparations for Death

How often have you heard it said after someone died: "Now they are in a better place"? Why don't we look forward to going to that better place while we are still alive? What are we afraid of? We should be looking forward to the time when we will leave our earthly existence and enter into the spiritual world. At one moment we are living an earthly existence, and then in the next moment, we open our eyes on eternity. How wonderful it will be to die and pass from this life into eternity! Do not fear pain or death. Remember the words of St. John Paul II: *"Be not afraid."*

There is a special blessing that a Catholic priest can offer after administering the Sacrament of the Sick. It is called the Apostolic Pardon.

The Apostolic Pardon (or blessing) is a plenary indulgence given in situations of danger of death, usually after the absolution of the Sacrament of

Penance (Reconciliation) and the sacrament of the Anointing of the Sick. The focus is on the remission of temporal punishment due to sin. The words of the prayer explain the meaning of the act:

"Through the holy mysteries of our redemption may almighty God release you from all punishments in this life and in the life to come. May He open to you the gates of paradise and welcome you to everlasting joy." Or "By the authority which the Apostolic See has given me, I grant you a full pardon and the remission of all your sins in the name of the Father, and of the Son, and of the Holy Spirit."

The Handbook of Indulgences, #28, states:
Priests who minister the sacraments to the Christian faithful who are in a life-and-death situation should not neglect to impart to them the Apostolic Blessing, with its attached indulgence. But if a priest cannot be present, holy mother Church lovingly grants such persons who are rightly disposed a plenary indulgence to be obtained in "articulo mortis," (at the approach of death), provided they regularly prayed in some way during their lifetime. The use of a crucifix or a cross is recommended in obtaining this plenary indulgence. In such a situation the three usual conditions required in order to gain a plenary indulgence are substituted for by the condition "provided they regularly prayed in some way." [Rev. Mark J. Gantley, JCL Apostolic Pardon 12/17/2007 EWTN.com]

In summary, when a loved one is ready to pass on or experiencing a life-threatening medical procedure, a priest should be called to administer the sacrament of the Anointing of the Sick and the Apostolic Pardon.

My Personal Experience with the Preparations for Death

Before I finished writing this book, I experienced a medical emergency which required open-heart bypass surgery.

Throughout my eighty years, I have experienced a number of exciting and happy spiritual events. This started with my First Holy Communion and was followed by my Confirmation, as well as by my first marriage, for which my wife and I received a papal blessing. Forty-two years later, my holy wife was called home by God. Several years later, I married another spiritual woman and received another papal blessing. What made all these events so special was that they all involved the Holy Sacraments of the Church!

What made my medical emergency special was that, in preparation for my open-heart surgery, I was blessed to have a priest hear my confession, which could have been my last. I also received the Sacrament of the Anointing of the Sick, also known as the Last Rites, and was then given the special indulgence known as the Apostolic Pardon. This is a special blessing from the Holy See for the remission of temporal punishment due to sin. Finally, I received Jesus in the Holy Eucharist before going into surgery.

> That was an exciting experience, preparing for my ultimate goal of passing from this earthly existence into the next life!

As the anesthesia was administered, I couldn't help but smile at the thought that the next time I opened my eyes, I might possibly see our Lord! It brought tears of joy to my eyes. Waking up in recovery, when I opened my eyes and saw the nurses, I experienced joy. I guessed the Lord was telling me that I would need to do more to help others before I would be given the privilege of going home to Heaven.

It was a great experience to have had all the formal preparations for passing from this earthly life into the spiritual world. I pray daily that I will be as prepared when the Father finally calls me home!

> St. Cyprian wrote, *"What an honor, what happiness, to depart joyfully from this world to go forth into glory in anguish and pain in one moment, to close the eyes and look on the world of men and in the next to open the eyes and then look on God and Christ when you're suddenly withdrawn from the earth to find yourself in the kingdom of heaven."*

Now, how great is that!

Happiness and Love

"This is the glorious duty of man, to pray and to love. To pray to God and to love God and to love your fellow man. If you pray and love, this is where a person's happiness lies." St. John Vianney

Jesus

"To know everything and not to know Jesus is to know nothing." St. Louis de Montfort

> St. Polycarp tells us: *"All who refuse to believe in Him, must answer to God for the very blood of His Son."*

Judgment

Jesus is our judge. He came to earth and lived among us as a Divine Person, like us in all things but sin. Who better to judge us than one who lived as one of us? However, Jesus always goes through God the Father on all His judgments.

> *CCC 1441 Only God forgives sins. Since he is the Son of God, Jesus says of himself, "The Son of man has authority on earth to forgive sins" and exercises this divine power: "Your sins are forgiven." Further, by virtue of His divine authority* **He gives this power to men to exercise in His name.** *[Priests!] (Bold added)*

Jesus Shows His Love for Us

The cross is the most ancient, powerful, and universal Christian symbol, especially the crucifix, which is the cross with the figure of the crucified Jesus Christ affixed to it.

The image of the cross alone is important, as we know from Good Friday. During Good Friday Passion services, the faithful process in reverence behind the cross. The priest proclaims, *"Behold the wood of the cross, on which hung the Savior of the world,"* and the faithful respond, *"Come, let us worship."* This "worship" of the Good Friday cross should also be demonstrated for the crucifixes and crosses we have in our homes, and those we wear or see in public. They should remind us of Christ's suffering for our sins and how much He and the Father love us.

The Sufferings of the Blessed Mother

Our Lady had many great joys as the mother of Jesus, but she also experienced much suffering. The great love she had for her Son caused her enormous suffering when she saw Jesus treated so cruelly by His enemies. Her heart was like an altar on Calvary as she offered up her beloved Son on our behalf. Mary is the Queen of Martyrs because she went through spiritual torments greater than the bodily agonies of the martyrs.

In Mary's life there were **seven sorrows** of great suffering. The **first sorrow** occurred when she took the Baby Jesus to the temple. There the prophet Simeon told her that a sword of suffering would pierce her heart. (This would occur when Jesus was put to death.) She experienced her **second sorrow** when she and St. Joseph had to flee to Egypt because Herod's soldiers were trying to kill Baby Jesus. The **third sorrow** came as Mary and Joseph searched three days in Jerusalem for Jesus. They finally found Him in the temple. Our Lady's **fourth sorrow** came when Jesus was whipped and crowned with thorns. Her **fifth sorrow** came as she watched Him nailed to the cross, and she suffered until His death on Calvary. The **sixth sorrow** occurred as our Lord's lifeless body was placed in her arms, and finally the **seventh sorrow** was when His body was placed in the tomb.

Mary did not pity herself or complain about her suffering. Instead, she offered her sorrows to God for our sake. She is our spiritual mother, and because she loves us dearly, she lovingly agreed to suffer along with Jesus, so that we might someday share her joy with Jesus in Heaven.

> Absolute love occurs when one offers their suffering for another's benefit!

In honor of Our Lady of Sorrows, we can offer up some small sacrifice without complaining, while at the same time remembering her Seven Sorrows and thanking her for her great love for us.

In Jesus' dying words on the cross, He gave His mother to all of us.

"'Woman, behold your son', then he said to his disciple, (and to us) 'behold your mother!'" (John 19:26-27)

> The Blessed Mother suffered greatly from the time she said "yes" to God. Mothers and grandmothers can go to the Blessed Mother and her mother, St. Anne, for understanding and solace during times of suffering for themselves or for their families. Fathers and grandfathers can go to St. Joseph and St. Joachim for understanding and solace while suffering family problems.

Is Suffering in This World Really All That Bad?

The Joyful Mysteries of the rosary were each preceded by sorrow or worry for the Blessed Mother. In the first Joyful Mystery, the Annunciation, the Angel Gabriel appeared to a teenage Mary and informed her that she had found favor with God, and that through the power of the Holy Spirit, she would conceive a son who would be the Savior of mankind. Put yourself in Mary's place. How would you tell your mother and father? How would you tell your husband that you are pregnant by the power of the Holy Spirit and that you found favor with God by a message from an angel?

According to tradition, Sts. Anne and Joachim both had visits from angels to announce that St. Anne would become pregnant with Mary. So they believed Mary when she told them about her visit from the Angel Gabriel. Until the angel visited Joseph in a dream and told him to take Mary as his wife, he was going to quietly divorce her. In the second Joyful Mystery,

A Journey to Holiness

the pregnant Mary visited her cousin Elizabeth. Did Joseph safely escort her to Elizabeth? Wouldn't her husband Joseph safely bring his young, pregnant wife to her cousin?

Their worries continued when Mary was close to delivering and they were required to go to Bethlehem to register for the census. What worries did they experience on that journey? Then they arrive in Bethlehem and there is no place to stay. How do you think Joseph felt? How worried was Mary? The third Joyful Mystery, the birth of Jesus, came in spite of those worries.

The fourth Joyful Mystery is the Presentation. Can you imagine how happy Mary and Joseph were to bring Jesus to the temple to be presented and blessed in accordance with Jewish custom? How did they feel when they met Simeon at the entrance to the temple, and he tells them that Jesus is the Redeemer he has waited for all his life, but also warns Mary that her heart will be pierced with a sword?

The fifth Joyful Mystery is the Finding of the Child Jesus in the Temple. Imagine how parents feel when they lose sight of a child in a store or a large crowd. Imagine how Mary and Joseph felt when they realized that Jesus was not in the caravan that was traveling back to their home. Imagine their worry, not knowing if Jesus was left behind in Jerusalem; or was lost on the road; sick; or worse yet, was kidnapped or dead? Even after they returned to Jerusalem, a large city, where would they begin to look for Him?

In the Joyful Mysteries we witness Mary's great joy, also keeping in mind how she suffered before each of these joys.

(See page 103 – "Why Does God Permit Evil in His Creation?")

Does God Hear Our Prayers When We Suffer?

Many times we may question if God actually hears our prayers. Many of the famous saints have also questioned God's friendship when He did not quickly respond to their requests for help. St. Teresa of Avila, out of frustration, once said to our Lord:

"Lord, if you treat your friends this way, it's no wonder you have so few of them!"

And Blessed Mother Teresa of Calcutta has said: "I know, Lord, that you don't give anyone more than they can handle, but sometimes I think you may have mistaken me for someone else."

The Holy Spirit Brings Us Closer to God Through Prayer

> *CCC 667 Jesus Christ, having entered the sanctuary of heaven once and for all, intercedes constantly for us as the mediator who assures us of the permanent outpouring of the Holy Spirit.*

You must be willing to accept the word of God through the Holy Spirit. Listen and pay attention to the words or ideas that come to you. The closer you become to God, and to the light of His wisdom, the more you can see yourself, your imperfections, and sins. For example, think of your soul as a pane of glass. When you are looking through the glass as it is turned away from the light, you cannot see any imperfections or dirt on the glass. As the glass turns toward the light, the imperfections become obvious. In the same way, the closer your soul gets to the light, the more visible your imperfections will become.

As believers get closer to God's light, they will see their sins and weaknesses more clearly. This is why many saintly people admit to being sinners, while others who are far from the light do not recognize their sinfulness. **One of the greatest benefits of praying frequently is the awareness of our sinfulness and the need for redemption.**

"[s]eek first the kingdom of God and his righteousness, and all these things will be given you besides." (Matthew 6:33)

> On May 7, 2014, during his weekly general audience, Pope Francis said: "Through the Holy Spirit, God is there to enlighten people's hearts and help us understand the right things to say, the right way to act and the right road to take, when it comes to important decisions. By opening one's heart to God, the Holy Spirit immediately begins to help us perceive His voice and guide our thoughts, our feelings and our intentions to be in harmony with God's will."

Our Sinfulness

We sin through commission and omission. Sins of commission are the actual sins we commit when we actively do something against God's laws. We can commit sins of omission when we fail to do something we ought to do, such as doing something good for our family, who we are directly responsible for, and for others who we may, through our conscience, need to help but did not.

"The Lord never tires of forgiving us. It is we who get tired of asking for pardon." Pope Francis (April 16, 2015)

Original Sin

We are all sinners by our very nature because of the sin of Adam and Eve. Their disobedience gave us original sin. We cannot escape sin, by word or deed. We have to admit before God that we are sinners, and we must repent for all we have done to be unfaithful to God.

Note: After we are baptized, original sin is taken away, but concupiscence **(our propensity to sin)** always remains with us. When we sin, we turn away from God our Creator and turn to Satan who wants us to be with him in hell!

Truth or Lies—God vs. Satan

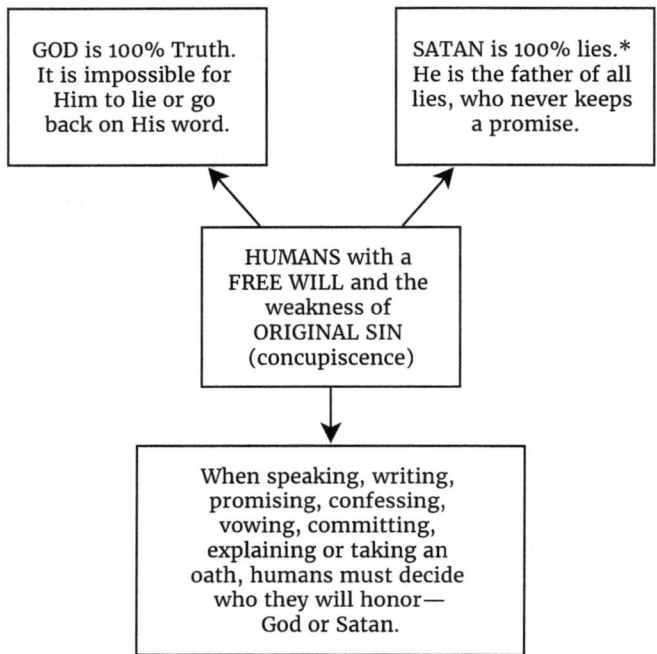

*While Satan sometimes tells the truth, his intention will always be to pull you into sin. The ultimate goal of his "truth" is evil.

We choose to honor and follow either God or Satan. The choice is always our decision because we have been given free will.

Every time we lie, we turn away from God and turn toward Satan. Any form of a lie is pleasing to Satan, because a lie is the opposite of the truth. Once Satan convinces you to justify little "white lies," he can then slowly work on you, convincing you to tell bigger lies.

Justifying the little "white lie" makes lying easier and ensures it becomes part of your lifestyle. When you continue to lie, you turn your back on God and turn to Satan. Any lie is an offense against the First Commandment: "Thou shall not have any strange gods before me." This means that if you are not 100% truthful, you don't totally trust God. Therefore, you do, at least in part, trust Satan more than God by your lies!

> If you don't give God 100% of your love and truthfulness, Satan takes the remaining percent of your love and truthfulness. Lies never end well. They are always rewarded with something "bad" from Satan, whereas God always rewards the truth.

Capital Sins

> *CCC 1866 Vices can be classified according to the virtues they oppose, or also be linked to the capital sins which Christian experience has distinguished, following St. John Cassian and St. Gregory the Great. They are called "capital" because they engender other sins, other vices.* **They are pride, avarice (greed), envy, wrath (anger), lust, gluttony, and sloth or acedia.** *(Bold added)*

"But I say to you, whoever is angry with his brother shall be liable to judgment." (Matthew 5:22)

> "The sin of anger and impatience has a unique aspect as it presents us with the greatest foretaste of hell in this life." St. Catherine of Siena

The Consequence of Sin

> CCC 1472 ...it is necessary to understand that sin has a double consequence. Grave sin deprives us of communion with God and therefore makes us incapable of eternal life, the privation of which is called the "eternal punishment" of sin. On the other hand every sin, even venial, entails an unhealthy attachment to creatures, which must be purified either here on earth, or after death in the state called Purgatory. This purification frees one from what is called the "temporal punishment" of sin. These two punishments must not be conceived of as a kind of vengeance inflicted by God from without, but as following from the very nature of sin. A conversion which proceeds from a fervent charity can attain the complete purification of the sinner in such a way that no punishment would remain.

The Stain of Sin

No one can enter into Heaven with any stain of sin on their soul. Imagine that every sin is a wet tea bag and your soul is a pure white silk pillow. When we sin, the wet tea bag puts a stain on our soul (the white silk pillow). When we go to confession and tell Jesus our sins through the priest, we are given absolution which removes the wet tea bag from the white silk pillow. The tea bag **(our sin)** is thrown away forever, but the stain remains on the pillow (our soul). We cannot enter Heaven with any stain of sin on our soul. Even after confession, when our sins are totally forgiven and taken away, the stain remains. It is in Purgatory that we can remove the "stain" of temporal punishment due to sin.

CCC 1473 The forgiveness of sin and restoration of communion with God entail the remission of the eternal punishment of sin, but temporal punishment of sin remains. While patiently bearing sufferings and trials of all kinds and, when the day comes, serenely facing death, the Christian must strive to accept this temporal punishment of sin as a grace. He should strive by works of mercy and charity, as well as by prayer and the various practices of penance, to put off completely the "old man" and to put on the "new man."

There are various ways in which we can remove the stain of sin while we are still living in this world: penance, good works, sacrifice, Divine Mercy prayers, partial and plenary indulgences. We can offer our earthly sufferings to God for the removal of our temporal punishment. Purgatory is the last opportunity we have to remove the stain of sin from our soul before we can enter into Heaven.

A Journey to Holiness

> *CCC 1031 The Church gives the name Purgatory to this final purification of the elect, which is entirely different from the punishment of the damned. The Church formulated her doctrine of faith on Purgatory especially at the Councils of Florence and Trent. The tradition of the Church, by reference to certain texts of Scripture, speaks of a cleansing fire:*
>
>> *As for certain lesser faults, we must believe that, before the Final Judgment, there is a purifying fire. He who is truth says that whoever utters blasphemy against the Holy Spirit will be pardoned neither in this age nor in the age to come. From this sentence we understand that certain offenses can be forgiven in this age, but certain others in the age to come.*
>
> *CCC 1498 Through indulgences the faithful can obtain the remission of temporal punishment resulting from sin for themselves and also for the souls in Purgatory.*

St. Nicholas of Tolentino is known as the patron saint of holy souls, the souls in Purgatory. We can pray to him to help us remove the stains we have accumulated over our lifetime that are on **our** soul or on the souls of our loved ones who might be in Purgatory!

Confession/Reconciliation

According to the Catechism, we should confess our mortal sins according to their type and kind and the approximate number of times they were committed. **We need not describe in detail the sins**, but only answer questions the priest may have, if he needs more details to understand the circumstances or the scope of the sin. **(The priest should not ask imprudent questions solely to satisfy a morbid curiosity. These are questions the penitent does not have to answer.)**

> Remember, during the sacrament of confession/reconciliation, you are talking directly to Jesus through the person of the priest.
>
> Look forward to having a private talk with Jesus about your imperfections and weaknesses in the confessional!

Jesus will judge us when we pass from this world to the next. He knows everything we do or think. There is no "fooling" Jesus. He wants us to be truthful in the confessional and to be truly sorry for our sins. Finally, He wants us to do penance in reparation for our sins. There isn't any sin that you can tell Him that He hasn't heard before.

One of the most memorable experiences I had during confession came after I had finished telling my sins to the priest (through whom Jesus is working.) That priest asked me to tell him all the good I had done since my last confession! Needless to say I was taken by surprise, and was not prepared to tell him the good I had done. I will always remember that priest. Now when I go to confession, I not only think of my sins, but I also think about the good I have done to help others, just in case the priest might ask me that same question. That memorable confession happened over fifty years ago and still affects me today.

In all those years I have never had any priest ask me that same question again.

The Significance of Three in Making Reparations

- The child Jesus was lost for three days.
- Jesus was in the tomb for three days before rising from the dead.
- Jesus suffered on the cross for three hours.
- Esther's command to fast three days and nights.
- Jonas was in the belly of the whale for three days.
- Joseph sent his brothers to jail for three days.
- The Israelites went without food or water for three days after Moses parted the Red Sea.

In reparation for our sins we can offer a three-week, three-day, or three-hour period of prayers and sacrifice during which we can offer up our suffering and problems. These offerings can help prepare us for a new level of spiritual change.

The Wonders of Heaven

How wonderful Heaven will be, when we will be privileged to know the inner thoughts and feelings of everyone who has ever lived on earth! Imagine being able to know the personal feelings between Jesus and His mother. What were her thoughts when she held Him as a baby? What did she say to Him? Did she sing to Him? What questions did Mary and Joseph ask Jesus as He was growing up? In Heaven we will be privileged to know all these details.

Recently, there were reports of a three-and-a-half-year-old boy who, during a serious medical operation, had a vision of Jesus and of some of the souls in Heaven. When questioned about the ages of the souls he met, including the miscarried sister his mother never told him about, and his grandfather who died before he was born, he said they were all about Jesus' age (thirty-three years old).

While the Catholic Church does not teach this as doctrine, it sounds logical to me. This assumption about the age of the saints in Heaven has been speculated about for many years.

> "We do not cease praying so long as we continue to do good. The prayer of the heart and of good deeds has more value than the prayer of the lips." St. Augustine

> "Prayer is the raising of the mind to God. We must always remember this. The actual words matter less."
> **Pope St. John XXIII**

CHAPTER 5

Spiritual Observations and Resources

"Give me an account of your service."
(Luke 16:2)

In this chapter, I share my spiritual observations and the resources that guided me throughout life, to better understand God's plan for me with the ultimate goal of attaining Heaven. Some of the subjects include: the importance of sincerity in prayer; self-evaluation questionnaires; and suggestions on how to keep a God-pleasing home. The resources I list are those I used to direct me on my journey, including the rosary and the Divine Mercy Chaplet, both of which have been recommended by all recent popes, from St. John Paul II to Pope Francis.

Spiritual Observations

Everything we have comes from God. All material goods—house, cars, all our worldly belongings—come from God. We are stewards of God's gifts to us, including our physical bodies and we are required to use these assets in a responsible Christian manner. God has also blessed us with our intellect, skills, and abilities, which we use to make a living, earning us the money we need to purchase the assets we accumulate. We are required to use our intellect, abilities, and assets in the same Christian manner.

The Gift of Time

> Our valuable earthly time could be offered as a spiritual gift of thanks to God. Everyone, whether rich, poor, young, or old, can afford to give God their time in thanksgiving for all His gifts which they have received.

Our earthly time does not exist in Heaven, but serves as a bridge between Heaven and earth. Time as we know it is a human and earthly reality, something of value that is measurable, and that we can spiritually give in thanksgiving to God, Jesus, the Holy Spirit, the Blessed Mother, and the saints. How else can I give thanks to God for all His gifts except to give Him my time?

FACTS:
- There is a GOD.
- There is a Heaven and a hell.
- Every human person has a soul.
- Every soul will exist for all eternity.
- Every soul will have to account for how they used the gifts and talents God blessed them with.
- Each soul will go to Heaven or hell for all eternity.

MORE FACTS: Below is a breakdown of how the average practicing Roman Catholic spends their 168-hour week (space has been provided for you to record your average week):

Average Catholic Activities Per Week		Your Hours
33.3% – 56 hrs.	Sleeping	
23.8% – 40 hrs.	Working	
20.8% – 35 hrs.	Watching television/computer	
8.3% – 14 hrs.	Eating	
4.1% – 7 hrs.	Traveling	
4.1% – 7 hrs.	Personal grooming	
2.3% – 4 hrs.	Personal activities	
2.3% – 4 hrs.	Daily prayer & rosary	
.6% – 1 hr.	Sunday Mass	
Weekly Total: 168 hrs.	Your Total:	

The average time per week spent for GOD is five hours or 3.0% of the total time available. If a person who claims they love you only spent 3.0% of their time for or with you, would you consider that love? When we love someone, we want to spend time with them. Most of all we sacrifice for them and go out of our way to please them! How much do we REALLY sacrifice for GOD?

What Must I Do to Gain Eternal Life?

It is our Lord's commandment that we love God with all of our heart, soul, mind, and all our strength, which means 100%; nothing less. What do we need to give to God 100%? This requires a serious examination of your heart, being completely honest with yourself. Have you been the very best parent, spouse, student, employee, parishioner, etc., that you could be in the eyes of God?

Each of us has been given special talents or qualities that should be used to carry out God's plan. If someone has a great intellect and becomes a teacher, they should use that talented gift to promote God's will and not their own prideful glory. Likewise, if they have been given the skills to be a good carpenter, they should build the best they can in thanksgiving for their gift from God. No one should be jealous of another person's talents particularly if they did not receive the same talents. Jealousy is a form of pride, because you believe you deserve better than you received.

> People buy insurance for their homes, their health, and possessions, even for their life. What kind of insurance do they have for their eternal soul?

Trust in God

Trust is a form of love for God the Father. A simple prayer of trust is *"Father, I Trust in You!" (Repeat three times.)*

The following is God's revelation to St. Faustina: *"The more a soul trusts, the more it will receive. Souls that trust boundlessly, are a great comfort to me because I pour all the treasures of my graces into them, I rejoice that they ask for much because it is my desire to give much, very much. I am sad when souls ask for little, when they narrow their hearts."* St. Faustina Diary 1578

"Let us ask God's help before doing anything. If we acted in this way, we would perform wonders, for it would be God's acting always in us." St. Peter Eymard

"Therefore, do not be anxious about tomorrow, for tomorrow will be anxious for itself. Let the day's own troubles be sufficient for the day." (Matthew 6:34)

"You shall receive power when the Holy Spirit has come upon you." (Acts 1:8)

> Another prayer of trust that I offer is, *"Lord God, help me to remember that yesterday is gone forever and tomorrow may never come. Let me live in the present and give you thanks for all you have blessed me with."*

We Are One Family

We were all made in the image and likeness of God; therefore, we should see everyone as equal. When we are praying, we should include everyone in our intentions, regardless of race, nationality, or religion as part of God's family. All are worthy of our prayers.

"At the evening of life, we will be judged on love, love of neighbor, love of God, love of the Church, love of Jesus." St. John of the Cross

"One must see God in everyone." St. Catherine Laboure

St. Augustine said, *"Since you do not yet see God, you merit the vision of God by loving your neighbor. By loving your neighbor you prepare your eyes to see God."*

Keeping a "God-Pleasing" Home

St. Augustine called the family home the *"Domestica Ecclesia,"* that is, the "Domestic Church."

The home is a sanctuary away from the pressures of the outside world, a place where we should feel safe from "bad" things. We install locks and other security devices to protect us from people who might do us harm. But how do we protect ourselves against spiritual harm? *Where God is, evil is not....Where evil is, God is not....* If God is not welcomed into our homes, He will not go there. He will not stay in an unholy environment. He has commanded us not to serve or honor any other gods, which means He expects to be our only God **(our priority)**. He has given us the resources to protect us from evil.

In the story of the first Passover, an angel instructed the faithful to rub the blood of a lamb on their door frames. The Angel of Death saw this as a sign of their faith and passed over their home, saving their sons. While we have not had an angel appear, giving us specific instructions, we should make sure our homes are pleasing to God who will protect us against spiritual harm from the evil one and his minions.

> Consider organizing with your family, friends, and fellow parishioners to have all your homes blessed and dedicated to Jesus and His mother, as a safe sanctuary away from the dangers of the secular world. There is an official "Sacred Heart Enthronement" to Jesus and the "Two Hearts Enthronement" to Jesus and Mary which are offered by the Church for your home. If you are interested, you can see your parish priest for details.

In my home I have a special religious front-door plaque, which is secured to the outside door frame just below the upper *(horizontal)* cross-beam, for easy visibility to all entering and exiting the home. I have also placed several religious statues outside my house as a visible sign that believers live in this house.

Before installing the plaques, pictures, or statues on the outside of the house or anywhere within the home, they were first blessed as a religious, holy sacramental by a priest.

Another suggestion is to set aside a special day of the year as a home-blessing day to be administered through your local parish. A celebration Mass can be offered with special prayers to Jesus, Mary, and St. Michael for a peaceful, blessed, protected home that is pleasing to God.

Spiritual Resources

The Holy Rosary

If you love Jesus, you will love the rosary, as the rosary is the story of Jesus and His mother!

Praying the Rosary

You don't have to be Catholic to recite the rosary!

There are only six prayers that make up a basic rosary, and there are twenty mysteries to meditate upon as you recite the six prayers.

Blessed Fulton Sheen has said, *"The rosary is the book of the blind, where souls see and enact the greatest drama of love the world has ever known; it is the book of the simple, which initiates them into mysteries and knowledge more satisfying than the education of other men; it is the book of the aged, whose eyes close upon the shadow of this world, and open on the substance of the next. The power of the rosary is beyond description."*

Our Lady has been known to answer many impossible intentions from those who are first learning to pray the rosary. This is her way of bringing people closer to her and Jesus. If you are praying your first rosary, or returning to the rosary after years of not talking to Our Lady, ask for something big, something you think is impossible. She will often surprise you.

Beginning to Pray the Rosary

You may say the rosary using rosary beads, but it is perfectly acceptable to count with your fingers. Counting the beads frees your mind and helps you meditate on the mysteries.

Begin a rosary by making the Sign of the Cross: *In the name of the Father, and of the Son, and of the Holy Spirit. Amen.*

Next recite the Apostles' Creed:

I believe in God, the Father Almighty, Creator of Heaven and earth; and in Jesus Christ, His only Son, our Lord, who was conceived by the Holy Spirit, born of the Virgin Mary, suffered under Pontius Pilate, was crucified, died, and was buried. He descended into hell; the third day He rose again from the dead; He ascended into Heaven, and sits at the right hand of God, the Father Almighty; from thence He shall come to judge the living and the dead. I believe in the Holy Spirit, the holy Catholic Church, the communion of saints, the forgiveness of sins, the resurrection of the body and life everlasting. Amen.

Next say one Our Father, three Hail Marys *(for the three theological virtues of faith, hope, and charity)* and then a Glory Be.

The Our Father

Our Father who art in Heaven, hallowed be Thy name. Thy Kingdom come. Thy will be done, on earth as it is in Heaven. Give us this day our daily bread, and forgive us our trespasses, as we forgive those who trespass against us. And lead us not into temptation, but deliver us from evil. Amen.

The Hail Mary

Hail Mary, full of grace, the Lord is with thee; blessed art thou among women, and blessed is the fruit of thy womb, Jesus. Holy Mary, Mother of God, pray for us sinners, now and at the hour of our death. Amen.

The Glory Be

Glory be to the Father, and to the Son, and to the Holy Spirit. As it was in the beginning, is now, and ever shall be, world without end. Amen.

The Mysteries of the Rosary

The rosary consists of four mysteries, each consisting of five decades. The four mysteries are the Joyful, Sorrowful, Glorious, and Luminous Mysteries.

The Joyful Mysteries
(Prayed on Mondays and Saturdays)

The First Joyful Mystery, **The Annunciation**: The Archangel Gabriel announces to the teenaged Mary that she has been chosen to conceive the Son of God, and she gives her *Fiat* (Latin for "Let it be").

The Second Joyful Mystery, **The Visitation**: The pregnant Mary visits her cousin Elizabeth, who was pregnant with John the Baptist. Elizabeth greets her saying, "Blessed are you among women and blessed is the child you will bear."

The Third Joyful Mystery, **The Nativity:** Jesus, the Son of God is born to the woman, Mary, through the power of the Holy Spirit in a stable in Bethlehem.

The Fourth Joyful Mystery, **The Presentation:** When Mary and Joseph go to the temple to present Jesus to God, in accordance with the custom of the time, they meet Simeon who tells them, "This child is destined to be the downfall and the rise of many in Israel." (Luke 2:34) *(And that Mary's heart would be pierced with a sword.)*

The Fifth Joyful Mystery, **The Finding of the Child Jesus in the Temple:** After losing Jesus on their journey home from Jerusalem, Mary and Joseph search for Him for three days, and find the young Jesus teaching the rabbis in the temple.

The Luminous Mysteries (also known as the Mysteries of Light) *(Prayed on Thursdays)*

The First Luminous Mystery, **The Baptism of Jesus in the River Jordan:** As Jesus is baptized by His cousin John, the voice of the Father declares Jesus as His beloved Son.

The Second Luminous Mystery, **Wedding Feast of Cana:** At the request of His mother, Jesus changes water into wine at the wedding feast. It is His first public miracle.

The Third Luminous Mystery, **The Proclamation of the Kingdom of Heaven and the Call to Conversion:** Jesus preaches about the Kingdom and in the Sermon on the Mount gives us the Beatitudes as a model for living.

The Fourth Luminous Mystery, **The Transfiguration:** Jesus is transfigured in the presence of Peter, James, and John on the mountaintop.

The Fifth Luminous Mystery, **The Institution of the Eucharist:** Jesus offers the first Mass during the Last Supper with His Apostles, during which He institutes the Holy Eucharist.

The Sorrowful Mysteries
(Prayed on Tuesdays and Fridays)

The First Sorrowful Mystery, **The Agony in the Garden:** Jesus sweats blood while praying the night before His Passion (i.e., the night of the arrest.)

The Second Sorrowful Mystery, **The Scourging at the Pillar:** Pilate has Jesus beaten and whipped.

The Third Sorrowful Mystery, **The Crowning with Thorns:** The Roman soldiers placed a crown of thorns on Jesus' head.

The Fourth Sorrowful Mystery, **Jesus Carries His Cross:** Jesus falls three times while carrying His cross on the way to Calvary.

The Fifth Sorrowful Mystery, **The Crucifixion:** Jesus is nailed to the cross and dies three hours later, in the presence of His mother, the Apostle John, and Mary Magdalene.

The Glorious Mysteries
(Prayed on Wednesdays and Sundays)

The First Glorious Mystery, **The Resurrection:** Jesus rises from the dead on Easter.

The Second Glorious Mystery, **The Ascension:** Jesus ascends into Heaven forty days after His resurrection.

The Third Glorious Mystery, **The Descent of the Holy Spirit**: The Holy Spirit, in the form of tongues of fire, descends upon Mary and the Apostles in the upper room.

The Fourth Glorious Mystery, **The Assumption**: The Blessed Mother is assumed body and soul into Heaven at the end of her life on earth.

The Fifth Glorious Mystery, **The Coronation**: The Blessed Mother is crowned Queen of Heaven and earth.

For each decade, meditate upon the particular mystery. Start each decade by praying one Our Father on the first large bead, then ten Hail Marys for each of the smaller beads. End with one Glory Be before beginning the next decade. Do this for each of the five decades.

After each decade, the Fatima Prayer may also be said:

"O my Jesus, forgive us our sins, save us from the fires of hell. Lead all souls into Heaven, especially those in most need of Thy mercy."

Concluding Rosary Prayers

After the completion of the five decades, the following prayer is customarily said:

"Hail, holy Queen, Mother of Mercy, our life, our sweetness, and our hope. To thee do we cry, poor banished children of Eve. To thee do we send up our sighs, mourning and weeping in this valley of tears. Turn then, most gracious advocate, thine eyes of mercy toward us, and after this, our exile, show us the blessed fruit of thy womb, Jesus. O Clement, O loving, O sweet Virgin Mary..."

Verse: *"Pray for us, O Holy Mother of God."*

Response: *"That we may be made worthy of the promises of Christ."*

This completes the rosary. *(Normally takes only 18–20 minutes.)*

> *"Never will anyone who says his rosary every day be led astray."* St. Louis de Montfort

Meditating on the Mysteries of the Rosary

Always try to place yourself in the scene of the particular mystery as you pray. Picture the sights, sounds, and emotions that Jesus, Mary, Joseph, and the Apostles experienced during the actual events. Additionally, try to meditate on the meaning of the words of the prayers as you pray them. Or you may meditate on the person or intentions for which you are offering the rosary.

> Note: Every time you pray a rosary, you should dedicate or offer the purpose of the prayers for someone in need, or for a particular request, for example, the pro-life cause, world peace, health issues, etc.

Offering the Rosary for the Intentions of the Holy Father

Catholics, who pray the rosary in a group or individually before the Blessed Sacrament, may gain a plenary indulgence under the usual conditions, which includes a prayer for the intentions of the Holy Father.

(For the intentions of the Holy Father: recite one Our Father, one Hail Mary, and one Glory Be.)

The Fifteen Promises of the Rosary

In the 13th century, St. Dominic and Blessed Alan de la Roche received the following promises from Our Lady for all those who faithfully pray the rosary.

1. To all those who shall pray my Rosary devoutly, I promise my special protection and great graces.
2. Those who shall persevere in the recitation of my Rosary will receive some special grace.
3. The Rosary will be a very powerful armor against hell; it will destroy vice, deliver from sin, and dispel heresy.
4. The Rosary will make virtue and good works flourish, and will obtain for souls the most abundant divine mercies. It will draw the hearts of men from the love of the world and its vanities, and will lift them to the desire of eternal things. Oh, that souls would sanctify themselves by this means.
5. Those who trust themselves to me through the Rosary will not perish.
6. Whoever recites my Rosary devoutly reflecting on the mysteries, shall never be overwhelmed by misfortune. He will not experience the anger of God nor will he perish by an unprovided death. The sinner will be converted; the just will persevere in grace and merit eternal life.

7. Those truly devoted to my Rosary shall not die without the sacraments of the Church.
8. Those who are faithful to recite my Rosary shall have during their life and in their death the light of God and the plenitude of his graces and will share in the merits of the blessed.
9. I will deliver promptly from purgatory souls devoted to my Rosary.
10. True children of my Rosary will enjoy great glory in Heaven.
11. What you shall ask through my Rosary you shall obtain.
12. To those who propagate my Rosary I promise aid in all their necessities.
13. I have obtained from my Son that all the members of the rosary confraternity shall have as their intercessors, in life and in death, the entire celestial court.
14. Those who recite my Rosary faithfully are my beloved children, the brothers and sisters of Jesus Christ.
15. Devotion to my Rosary is a special sign of predestination.

Taken from "Fifteen Promises of the Rosary," CatholiCity.com

The Divine Mercy Chaplet

During the 1930s the Lord provided a Polish nun with many revelations. Along with these revelations which she recorded in her diary, **St. Faustina Kowalska was given a powerful prayer that Jesus**

wanted everyone to say, The Chaplet of Divine Mercy, and He promised special graces to those who would recite it.

> "Whoever will recite it will receive great mercy at the hour of death." (Diary, #687)

> "Priests will recommend it to sinners as their last hope of salvation. Even if there were a sinner most hardened, if he were to recite this chaplet only once, he would receive grace from My infinite mercy." (Diary, #687)

> "I desire to grant unimaginable graces to those souls who trust in My mercy." (Diary, #1059)

> "When they say this chaplet in the presence of the dying, I will stand between My Father and the dying person not as the just judge, but as the merciful Savior." (Diary, #1541)

St. Faustina received a message of mercy from the Lord and was told to spread it throughout the world, which she has done. Sister Faustina is now recognized as a saint by the Church, and her diary, *Divine Mercy in My Soul*, has become the handbook for devotion to the Divine Mercy.

Reciting the Chaplet of Divine Mercy

Using ordinary rosary beads, begin by saying one Our Father, one Hail Mary, and one Apostles' Creed on the first three beads.

Next, on the first large bead before each decade recite:

"Eternal Father, I offer you the body and blood, soul and divinity, of your dearly beloved Son, our Lord, Jesus Christ, in atonement for our sins and those of the whole world."

Then on each of the ten small beads of the decade, say:

"For the sake of His sorrowful Passion, have mercy on us and on the whole world."

After reciting these prayers for each of the five decades, conclude with:

"Holy God, Holy Mighty One, Holy Immortal One, have mercy on us and on the whole world." (Recite 3 times.)

Optional closing prayer:

"Eternal God, in whom mercy is endless and the treasury of compassion inexhaustible, look kindly upon us and increase Your mercy in us, that in difficult moments we might not despair nor become despondent, but with great confidence submit ourselves to Your holy will, which is love and mercy itself. Amen."

The chaplet is complete. *(This will normally take 8–10 minutes.)*

Three O'Clock Prayer to the Divine Mercy

Jesus also revealed special ways to live out the response to His mercy. The first of these is to recite the Chaplet of Divine Mercy both as a novena and as a prayer for the three o'clock hour, the hour of His death.

"The Lord told me to say the Chaplet for nine days before the Feast of Mercy. It is to begin on Good Friday. **By this novena I will grant every possible grace to souls.**" (Diary # 796)

Jesus' central message to St. Faustina was His invitation for each of us to re-live His Passion during the three o'clock hour, while asking His mercy for ourselves and the whole world.

The actual three o'clock prayer: *"O Blood and Water, which gushed forth from the Heart of Jesus as a fount of Mercy for us, I trust in You."* (Diary, #84)

The following is Jesus talking to Sister Faustina:
"At three o'clock, implore my mercy, especially for sinners; and, if only for a brief moment, immerse yourself in My Passion, particularly in My abandonment at the moment of agony." **[When his disciples fell asleep and could not stay awake with Him!]** *"This is the hour of great mercy... In this hour, I will refuse nothing to the soul that makes a request of Me in virtue of My Passion."* (Diary, #1320) **(At each 3:00 AM or PM hour, remember Jesus as He suffered in the Garden of Gethsemane.)**

"As often as you hear the clock strike the third hour, immerse yourself completely in My mercy, adoring and glorifying it; invoke its omnipotence for the whole world, and particularly for poor sinners; for at that moment mercy was opened wide for every soul. In this hour you can obtain everything for yourself and for others for the asking; it was the hour of grace for the whole world—mercy triumphed over justice." (Diary, #1572)

"My daughter, try your best to make the Stations of the Cross in this hour, provided that your duties permit it; and if you are not able to make the Stations of the Cross, then at least step into the chapel for a moment and adore, in the Most Blessed Sacrament, My Heart, which is full of mercy; **and should you be unable to step into the chapel, immerse**

yourself in prayer there where you happen to be, if only for a very brief instant." (Diary, #1572)

St. Faustina also recorded Christ's words in which He emphasized that no one should be afraid to approach His mercy, no matter how extensive or grave their sins might be: *"Let no soul fear to draw near to me, even though its sins be as scarlet,"* (Diary, 699) and *"My mercy is greater than your sins and those of the entire world."* (Diary, #1485) Like a good physician wishing to spare his patients' sufferings, bring Him also your guilt, your sorrow, your difficulties, your addictions, and your physical illness, and unite them with His wounds, for as Christ stated to Faustina, *"No soul that has called upon my mercy has ever been disappointed or brought to shame."* (Diary, #1541)

Now How Great is That Promise?

The Beatitudes—A Roadmap to Holiness and Joy

CCC 1716 The Beatitudes are at the heart of Jesus' preaching during His Sermon on the Mount. They are the promises made to the chosen people. The Beatitudes fulfill God's promises by ordering them no longer merely to the possession of a territory, but to the Kingdom of Heaven:

1. *Blessed are the poor in spirit, for theirs is the kingdom of Heaven.*
2. *Blessed are those who mourn, for they shall be comforted.*

3. Blessed are the meek, for they shall inherit the earth.
4. Blessed are those who hunger and thirst for righteousness, for they shall be satisfied.
5. Blessed are the merciful, for they shall obtain mercy.
6. Blessed are the pure in heart, for they shall see God.
7. Blessed are the peacemakers, for they shall be called sons of God.
8. Blessed are those who are persecuted for righteousness' sake, for theirs is the kingdom of Heaven.
9. Blessed are you when men revile you and persecute you and utter all kinds of evil against you falsely on My account.
Rejoice and be glad,
for your reward is great in Heaven.

How wonderful are Jesus' promises to us!

The Seven Sacraments

The Baltimore Catechism defines a sacrament as **"an outward sign, instituted by Christ, to give grace."** Roman Catholics have seven sacraments. The sacraments have the power of giving grace through the merits of Jesus Christ. Some of the sacraments give sanctifying grace, and others *increase* it in our souls. Baptism and Reconciliation give sanctifying grace because they take away the stain of sin on our souls.

Holy Communion, Confirmation, Matrimony, Holy Orders, and the Anointing of the Sick *increase* sanctifying grace because those who receive them worthily are already living the life of grace. The sacraments always give grace, if we receive them with the right dispositions.

> *CCC 1210 Christ instituted the sacraments of the new law. There are seven:* **1) Baptism, 2) Confirmation (or Chrismation), 3) the Eucharist, 4) Penance/Reconciliation, 5) the Anointing of the Sick, 6) Holy Orders,** *and* **7) Matrimony.** *The seven sacraments touch all the stages and all the important moments of Christian and human life: they give birth and increase, healing and mission to the Christian's life of faith. There is thus a certain resemblance between the stages of natural life and the stages of the spiritual life.*
>
> *CCC 1211 ...the sacraments form an organic whole in which each particular sacrament has its own vital place. In this organic whole, the Eucharist occupies a unique place as the "Sacrament of sacraments": "all the other sacraments are ordered to it as to their end."*

The Seven Sacraments (A Synopsis)

Definition of a Sacrament: "A Sacrament is an outward, visible sign instituted by Jesus Christ that gives the grace it signifies."

Three Sacraments of Initiation

1. **Baptism** takes away original sin and all personal sin while uniting us to Christ and His people. (A common symbol: Seashell pouring out Holy Water)
2. **Confirmation** deepens our union with Christ and helps us proclaim our faith in Him before others. (A common symbol: Holy Spirit as hovering dove)
3. **The Holy Eucharist** gives us the body and blood, soul and divinity of Jesus as our daily spiritual food to nourish our union with Him. (A common symbol: Consecrated Host suspended over chalice)

Two Sacraments of Union (at the service of Communion and Mission)

1. **Matrimony** makes a man and woman husband and wife and gives them grace to live with God, for God and each other. (A common symbol: Two rings intertwined)
2. **Holy Orders** gives a man the power of sacramental ministry and uniting or re-uniting believers with God as a deacon, priest, or bishop. Priests and bishops offer the Holy Sacrifice of the Mass. (Symbol: Book of Gospels, overlaid with priestly stole and ciborium)

Two Sacraments of Healing

1. **Confession** restores our union with Christ which has been disrupted by personal sins. (A common symbol: Crossed keys, to show the power of "binding and loosing")
2. The **Anointing of the Sick** heals and strengthens our union with Christ during times of serious illness. (A common symbol: Cruet of holy oil or hourglass)

God's Ten Commandments

1. I am the Lord your God: you shall not have strange gods before me.
2. You shall not take the name of the Lord your God in vain.
3. Remember to keep holy the Lord's Day.
4. Honor your father and your mother.
5. You shall not kill.
6. You shall not commit adultery.
7. You shall not steal.
8. You shall not bear false witness against your neighbor.
9. You shall not covet your neighbor's wife.
10. You shall not covet your neighbor's goods.

Spiritual Observations and Resources

The Fourteen Works of Mercy

- Seven corporal works of mercy
- Seven spiritual works of mercy

The Corporal Works

(Our charitable duty toward our neighbors' physical well-being)
1. Feed the hungry
2. Give drink to the thirsty
3. Clothe the naked
4. Visit the imprisoned
5. Shelter the homeless
6. Visit the sick
7. Bury the dead

The Spiritual Works

(Our charitable duty for the well-being of our neighbors' soul)
1. Admonish the sinner
2. Instruct the ignorant
3. Counsel the doubtful
4. Comfort the sorrowful
5. Bear wrongs patiently
6. Forgive all injuries done to you
7. Pray for the living and the dead

The Three Eminent Good Works in Christianity

1. **Prayer** – devoting time for spiritual words, study, or communication with God and His saints
2. **Fasting** – self-sacrifice of food or pleasure
3. **Almsgiving** – works of charity

Devotion to the Sacred Heart of Jesus

Jesus appeared to St. Margaret Mary Alacoque many times, during which He revealed to her the devotions to His Sacred Heart. The most special apparitions took place between 1673 and 1675. In one of these apparitions, Jesus said: *"Look at this Heart which has loved people so much, and yet they do not want to love Me in return. **Through you My divine Heart wishes to spread its love everywhere on earth.**"*

Jesus made at least twelve promises to St. Margaret Mary, telling her how He would help those who honor His Sacred Heart. These are:

1. I will give them all the graces necessary for their state in life.
2. I will establish peace in their families.
3. I will console them in all their troubles.
4. They shall find in My Heart an assured refuge during life and especially at the hour of their death.
5. I will pour abundant blessings on all their undertakings.

6. Sinners shall find in My Heart the source of an infinite ocean of mercy.
7. Tepid souls shall become fervent.
8. Fervent souls shall speedily rise to great perfection.
9. I will bless the homes where an image of My Heart shall be exposed and honored.
10. I will give to priests the power of touching the most hardened hearts.
11. Those who propagate this devotion shall have their names written in My Heart, never to be effaced.
12. The all-powerful love of My Heart will grant to those who shall receive Communion on the First Friday* of nine consecutive months, the grace of final repentance; they shall not die under my displeasure, nor without receiving their sacraments; My Heart shall be their assured refuge at that last hour.

*(The nine Fridays should be made in honor of His Sacred Heart. This means practicing the devotion and having a great love of His Sacred Heart, and must include receiving Communion at Holy Mass.)

St. Margaret Mary Alacoque was born in Burgundy, France, on July 22, 1647. She died suddenly on October 17, 1690.

On May 13, 1920, St. Margaret Mary was canonized by Benedict XV. Her incorrupt heart and brain were preserved in wax and a metal figurine of her body can be seen in the convent chapel of the Order of the Visitation in Paray, France.

A Journey to Holiness

The Stations of the Cross

The Stations of the Cross commemorate the fourteen key events of Holy Week. The majority of the events concern Jesus' final walk through the streets of Jerusalem carrying the cross. The prayers of the Stations are said in memory of Christ's suffering and crucifixion and can be said at any time throughout the year, not just during the Lenten season.

The Stations of the Cross are typically displayed along the walls inside Catholic churches. They help the faithful to focus on the sufferings of Christ during His Passion. Many of the Catholic faithful are devoted to the Stations of the Cross and can be seen "walking and praying the stations" before or after Mass.

Prayers that are said at the beginning of the Stations and then at each individual station are specific prayers which remind us what Jesus suffered at that time. There are various devotional booklets that feature these prayers.

(There are typically pictures or sculptures depicting the fourteen Stations.)

The 1st station: Jesus is condemned to death.

The 2nd station: Jesus carries His cross.

The 3rd station: Jesus falls the first time.

The 4th station: Jesus meets His mother.

The 5th station: Simon of Cyrene helps Jesus carry His Cross.

The 6th station: Veronica wipes the face of Jesus.

The 7th station: Jesus falls the second time.

The 8th station: Jesus meets the women of Jerusalem.

The 9th station: Jesus falls the third time.

The 10th station: Jesus is stripped of His garments.

The 11th station: Jesus is nailed to the cross.

The 12th station: Jesus dies on the cross.

The 13th station: Jesus is taken down from the cross and placed in the arms of His mother.

The 14th station: Jesus is laid in the tomb (sepulcher).

There is a plenary indulgence that may be obtained by praying the Stations of the Cross. (When all the usual conditions are followed for a plenary indulgence.)

A Prayer for Our Pastor and Shepherd

Fr. Joseph Mary Wolfe, M.F.V.A.
(A suggested prayer for a pastor that could be in the weekly church bulletin to remind parishioners to pray for their priest)

"Lord Jesus, Eternal High Priest, we worship you, our Head! We thank you for our pastor who shares in Your one Priesthood, who acts in Your stead, and who is the instrument of bringing Your Presence to us. Strengthen him, Lord, in times of trial, be his consolation in times of loneliness and give him the joy of seeing the fruits of his labors. I will pray for him and assist him as I am able, for You bring many graces and blessings to me through him. Amen."

EWTN Family Prayer Book
by Fr. Joseph Mary Wolfe, M.F.V.A.
—Used with Permission

"Family, a prayer that we pray together is a powerful prayer." Fr. Joseph Wolfe

A Prayer for Our Family

Mother Teresa of Calcutta

Heavenly Father, You have given us the model of life in the Holy Family of Nazareth.

Help us, O Loving Father, to make our family another Nazareth where love, peace and joy reign.

May it be deeply contemplative, intensely Eucharistic, revived with joy.

Help us to stay together in joy and sorrow in family prayer.

Teach us to see Jesus in the members of our families, especially in their distressing disguise.

May the Eucharistic Heart of Jesus make our hearts humble like His and help us to carry out our family duties in a holy way.

May we love one another as God loves each one of us, more and more each day, and forgive each other's faults as You forgive our sins.

Help us, O Loving Father, to take whatever You give and give whatever You take with a big smile.

Immaculate Heart of Mary, cause of our joy, pray for us.

St. Joseph, pray for us.
Holy Guardian Angels, be always with us, guide and protect us.
Amen.

> Remember the famous statement by Father Patrick Peyton: "The family that prays together stays together."

A Prayer for Grandparents

Pope Emeritus Benedict XVI

Lord Jesus, You were born of the Virgin Mary, the daughter of Saints Joachim and Anne.

Look with love on grandparents throughout the world.

Protect them! They are a source of enrichment for families, for the Church and for all of society. Support them!

As they grow older, may they continue to be, for their families, strong pillars of Gospel faith, guardians of noble domestic ideals and living treasures of sound religious traditions.

Make them teachers of wisdom and courage, so that they may pass on to future generations the fruits of their mature human and spiritual experience.

Lord Jesus, help families and society to value the presence and roles of grandparents. May they never be ignored or excluded, but always encounter respect and love.

Help them to live serenely and to feel welcomed in all the years of life that you give them.

Mary, Mother of all the living, keep grandparents constantly in your care, accompany them on their earthly pilgrimage and, by your prayers, grant that all families may one day be reunited in our Heavenly homeland, where you await all humanity for the great embrace of life without end.

Amen!

Elderly people often state that they don't accomplish much in their old age! But they have a special grace to offer powerful prayers for their children, grandchildren, and relatives, as well as for the spiritual support of their friends and their family members, the Church, society, government, and for the world. Many close elderly friends have lists of requests from their friends and families that are in need of prayers and offer their prayers daily either after Mass or at home together with their spouses.

Two Love Stories of Elderly Couples

(Who were blessed with a child late in life, and well past their childbearing years)

St. Anne and St. Joachim

St. Anne was born in Bethlehem and married St. Joachim from Nazareth in Galilee. St. Joachim was a wealthy livestock owner who was given the task of supplying the Temple of Jerusalem with sheep for sacrifices.

After twenty years of a holy prayerful marriage, Anne and Joachim had no children. Because the high priest believed their failure to produce offspring indicated a lack of God's heavenly blessing, Joachim's annual sacrifice and contribution to the temple was refused.

Joachim was discouraged and depressed when he overheard the temple-goers ridiculing him and Anne because of their childless state. Remembering that in answer to Abraham's prayers, God granted Abraham and his wife Sara a child late in life, it is said that Joachim went into the desert to plead with God for a child. He promised God that he would go into the desert to pray and fast for forty days. After he fulfilled his promise, the Archangel Gabriel appeared to assure Joachim that he and Anne would be blessed with a child. They were to name the girl "Mary" and dedicate her to God.

While Joachim was away praying in the desert, Anne was worried about her husband and wondered when he would return. In despair of her barren state, she prayed fervently. One day, while in her garden, she watched newborn birds in their nests and cried out, "Why was I born, Lord?" At that moment the Archangel Gabriel appeared to tell her she would soon give birth to a daughter whom she was to name Mary. Gabriel promised that the child she would bear would be blessed through the ages.

Though advanced in years, St. Joachim and St. Anne trusted God and remained fervent in their prayers to conceive a child. God was pleased with their devotion to Him and to each other, and chose to bless them with a **miraculous conception** as they were long past their childbearing years.

After her vision with the Archangel Gabriel, Anne rushed to share her excitement with her husband as he was returning back from the desert. She greeted him at the "Golden Gate" only to learn that he too was blessed with an angelic vision proclaiming the same good tidings. Tradition tells us that when they met and embraced at the Golden Gate, Anne conceived and was blessed with a miraculous conception as promised by the Archangel Gabriel. Their baby would be "the Immaculate Virgin Mary, born without original sin" who would become the mother of Jesus.

What an indescribable sweet happiness must have existed in their hearts to know God granted them such a blessing!

When she was just three years old, Sts. Anne and Joachim delivered Mary to the service of the Temple of Jerusalem in gratitude and devotion to God. She remained there through much of her childhood. When Mary was fourteen they betrothed her to Joseph of Nazareth, and her story continues with the birth of her Son Jesus, and His life on earth as the Savior of mankind.

This was a love story of an elderly couple who never lost faith that God would answer their prayers. Their devotion resulted in God blessing the world with the birth of our Savior!

The story of St. Anne's life and her connection to mankind as the holy mother of Mary and grandmother of Jesus was very popular to early Christians. In the year 550 A.D., a church was built in honor of St. Anne in Jerusalem, and it is believed to be near where Anne, Joachim, and Mary lived.

Since the 7th century, the Greek and Russian churches have celebrated feasts honoring Sts. Joachim and Anne. The Western churches began to celebrate the feast of St. Anne in the 16th century. The feast of Sts. Anne and Joachim is celebrated on July 26.

As a result of her exemplary love, devotion, and obedience to the will of God, St. Anne was named patroness of mothers, grandmothers, grandparents, unmarried women, infertile women, and unborn children. She is shown in art as a loving mother to Mary, often in the company of her beloved husband, St. Joachim, and many times with the Infant Jesus. St. Joachim is the patron of grandfathers.

Note: *Mary was miraculously conceived and born without the stain of original sin. This established her as the pure tabernacle of Jesus, whom she conceived by the Holy Spirit. December 8 is the Solemnity of the Immaculate Conception of the Blessed Virgin Mary, which commemorates how Mary was conceived without sin in the womb of St. Anne.*

August 15, the Solemnity of the Assumption of the Blessed Virgin Mary, commemorates the special privilege bestowed on Mary, Mother of Jesus, when she was assumed (taken up), body and soul, into the glory of Heaven. The Son of God began His human life in Mary's pure womb. It was fitting, then, that God would glorify her body as soon as her life here on earth was ended. Mary's Assumption is Catholic dogma, proclaimed by Pope Pius XII on November 1, 1950.

Elizabeth and Zachary

St. John the Baptist was miraculously conceived by Elizabeth, the elderly cousin of the Blessed Mother. She was told by the Angel Gabriel that she would conceive a child in her old age, and that the child would be a boy, to be given the name of John. Because Elizabeth's husband Zachary did not believe the Angel Gabriel's message, God punished Zachary by striking him mute. His ability to speak would return only after the fulfillment of the Lord's promise with the birth of John the Baptist.

St. John the Baptist was a great prophet. He announced Jesus as Lord, and prepared the people to be His followers. Let's all listen to St. John the Baptist's advice today and allow Jesus to become more and more important in our daily lives.

Conclusion

Both St. Anne and St. Joachim, and St. Elizabeth and Zachary, had a deep love for each other and for God. They shared an active faith and prayer life. Their love stories are examples of holy elderly couples who were given a great gift from God. Each couple was blessed with a miraculous conception which produced a great prophet, as well as an immaculate conception which gave mankind the mother of our Savior, Jesus Christ.

When a powerful love-relationship exists between an elderly husband and wife, and is coupled with a powerful prayer life and a love for God, the result can be miraculous! **Don't underestimate the power of love and prayer by the elderly!**

Note: *Miraculous Conception is regarded as a conception brought about by supernatural intervention, transcending the laws of nature.*

*The Immaculate Conception, in the Roman Catholic Church, is the doctrine that the Virgin Mary's soul was free from the stain of original sin from the moment of her soul's conception **(in the womb of St. Anne).***

(Contrary to popular misunderstanding, the term does NOT refer to the conception of Jesus Christ in the Virgin Mary's womb.)

Some other saints who had elderly parents include: St. Rita of Cascia, St. Stanislaus, St. Roch, St. Remigius, and St. Euphrosyne.

Don't forget about Abraham and Sara, who had their son Isaac in their "old age!"

> *"I will not be leaving my children, grandchildren, and great-grandchildren earthly wealth, but I pray that my spiritual wealth will be their inherence for all eternity!"*
> Raymond John Colvin

Epilogue

I thank Jesus for the many priests, deacons, and theologians who helped me to understand how I should pray and serve God. It was through their homilies at Mass, and by their instruction on religious programs in the media, that I built my prayer life. I owe them an eternity of thanks. (See page 171 – "A Prayer for Our Pastor and Shepherd") All I can promise is to remember them at daily Mass and in my Communion intentions.

I am also forever grateful to all my faithful friends and family for their examples of brotherly love while we are on our journey to Heaven.

I admire the love my non-Catholic friends and family members have for their fellow man and how they live a life of love and service. I especially admire their service to one another as they follow Jesus' example of love. I pray that one day they will be able to experience a special personal relationship with Jesus by receiving Him in the Holy Eucharist, just as Catholics experience the body, blood, soul, and divinity of Jesus at the Holy Mass. I pray they will one day also experience the honor and joy of being spiritually elevated into Heaven while united to Jesus, and being able to thank God for all the blessings they received while here on earth.

"When someone you love is alive and living in this world today, you can only be with them when they are physically in your presence—when they die, you can now be with them spiritually 24/7 as God will allow through your prayers."
Raymond John Colvin

Where Are You Going?

A certain popular priest often ends his homilies by asking the question, "Where are you going?" To which the congregation responds, "To Heaven!"

Outside church, while in public, the same priest asks his favorite question when greeting any of his parishioners: "And where are you going?"

I shall never forget that priest or where I am going. It's one of the reasons I had to write this book: to help others get to Heaven, which was this priest's intention for his parishioners.

My eighty years of religious and spiritual experiences have guided me throughout my life. I pray that the insights I have shared in this book may assist you on your journey to holiness and to Heaven. Only you can answer the priest's question: "Where are you going?"

> My parting words to my dying wife in the hospital were, **"See you in Heaven."**

Thank you, Jesus!
(A popular phrase used by my friend, Deacon William Steltemeier.)

Look Forward to Going to Heaven!

If you can recall the most joyful, pleasurable experience you ever had in this world, it wouldn't even represent one tiny grain of sand in the universe compared to the joy in Heaven.

Our human minds are not capable of understanding and visualizing how beautiful and joyful Heaven will be!

But, the ultimate experience will be to see the most beautiful and LOVING vision of God's face for all eternity and to hear these words:

"Well done, my good and faithful servant.... Come, share your master's joy." (Matthew 25:21)

Now, how awesome would that be?

"See you in Heaven."

> "To one who has faith,
> no explanation is necessary.
> To one without faith,
> no explanation is possible."
> *St. Thomas Aquinas*

Index of Chapter Subjects

CHAPTER 1
How and Why People Pray

How Do People Pray? :: 5
The Holy Spirit's Inspirations When Praying :: 7
Pray Through the Holy Spirit to Jesus :: 9
The Worldly Life vs. the Spiritual Life :: 10
God's Love for Us :: 11
What Is Love? :: 12
Free Will :: 14
We Cannot Pray or Work Our Way to Heaven :: 15
God's Grace and Final Judgment :: 16
What Can We Do to Please God? :: 17
What Is Prayer? :: 19
God's Plan for You :: 21
The Mission of My Life :: 22
Who is a God-Pleasing Person? :: 23
God's Plan Before and After Original Sin :: 24
How Much Does God Love Us? :: 25
The Eleventh Commandment :: 25

CHAPTER 2
Spiritual Motivations and Preparations

Prayer :: 27
Routine Prayer :: 29
Vocal Prayer :: 32
Meditation Prayer :: 32
Contemplative Prayer :: 33
People Who Have Influenced My Prayer Life :: 34
Accepting the Spiritual World :: 35
Our Spiritual and Earthly Families :: 38
Different Forms of Prayer :: 39
Opportunities for Prayer :: 41
Upon Waking in the Middle of the Night :: 42
Give God Your Best, Not Your Leftovers! :: 44
The Blessed Mother and Our Spiritual Family :: 46
My Spiritual Family :: 49
My Guardian Angel :: 49
The Sincerity of Prayer :: 50

CHAPTER 3
A Lifetime of Praying

A Brief Overview of How My Personal Prayer Life Evolved Over Eighty Years :: 54
The Value of Time When Praying :: 58
Praying Through and to the Saints :: 59
The Prayer That Jesus Taught Us :: 60
Growth of Prayer in the Stations of Life :: 61
God Never Sends Anyone to Hell :: 62

Index of Chapter Subjects

The Importance of a Routine Prayer Life :: 63
A Suggested Daily Prayer Routine :: 64
The Most Formal Prayer Is the Holy Mass :: 67
A Brief Overview of My Typical Daily
    Prayer Routine :: 68
My Additional Prayers and Activities :: 69
Prayer Spaces I Have Created :: 72
Details of My Daily Prayers :: 73
Preparing for Daily and Sunday Mass :: 79
My Specific Private Prayers at Holy Mass :: 81
Praying During Dark Days and Difficult Times :: 97
A Prayer to Jesus When Taking
    Strong Medications :: 100
Our Dark Days Bring Us Closer to God :: 102
Why Does God Permit Evil In His Creation? :: 103

CHAPTER 4
Inspirations and Beliefs

Life and Suffering :: 105
Our Eternal Soul :: 106
God's Love for Us :: 107
The Extent to Which God Loves Us :: 108
God's Will for Us :: 108
God Gives Us Examples of How We
    Can Please Him :: 109
God Gives Us the Resources to Help Us
    on Our Journey to Heaven :: 110
The Communion of Saints :: 111
God's Laws :: 113

Offering Your Service to God :: 114

Putting Self Before God :: 114

You Cannot Love God If You Are Thinking About Yourself! :: 114

Love for God and Neighbor :: 115

God Talks to Us :: 116

Thanking God for Marital Relations :: 116

Make God Part of Your Daily Life :: 117

God's Plan for Us :: 117

Giving Thanks :: 118

Giving God Thanks for Allowing Suffering :: 118

Jesus' Love for Us :: 119

For Those of Faith: The Historical Evidence for the Real Presence of Jesus in the Eucharist :: 119

Being Lukewarm :: 120

Faith and Suffering :: 120

Developing a Formal Prayer Life :: 121

The Church Encourages Continual Prayer :: 121

Preparations for Death :: 122

My Personal Experience with the Preparations for Death :: 124

Happiness and Love :: 126

Jesus :: 126

Judgment :: 126

Jesus Shows His Love for Us :: 127

The Sufferings of the Blessed Mother :: 127

Is suffering in this world really all that bad? :: 129

Does God Hear Our Prayers When We Suffer? :: 131

The Holy Spirit Brings Us Closer to
  God Through Prayer :: 131
Our Sinfulness :: 133
Original Sin :: 133
Truth or Lies—God vs. Satan :: 134
Capital Sins :: 135
The Consequence of Sin :: 136
The Stain of Sin :: 136
Confession/Reconciliation :: 138
The Significance of Three in Making
  Reparations :: 140
The Wonders of Heaven :: 140

CHAPTER 5
Spiritual Observations and Resources

Spiritual Observations :: 144
The Gift of Time :: 144
What Must I Do to Gain Eternal Life? :: 146
Trust in God :: 147
We Are One Family :: 148
Keeping a "God-Pleasing" Home :: 148
Spiritual Resources :: 150
The Holy Rosary :: 150
The Fifteen Promises of the Rosary :: 157
The Divine Mercy Chaplet :: 158
Reciting the Chaplet of Divine Mercy :: 159
Three O' Clock Prayer to the Divine Mercy :: 160
The Beatitudes—A Roadmap to Holiness and Joy :: 162
The Seven Sacraments :: 163

The Seven Sacraments (A Synopsis) :: 164
God's Ten Commandments :: 166
The Fourteen Works of Mercy :: 167
The Three Eminent Good Works in Christianity :: 168
Devotion to the Sacred Heart of Jesus :: 168
The Stations of the Cross :: 170
A Prayer for Our Pastor and Shepherd :: 171
A Prayer for Our Family :: 172
A Prayer for Grandparents :: 173
Two Love Stories of Elderly Couples :: 175
St. Anne and St. Joachim :: 175
Elizabeth and Zachary :: 178
Conclusion :: 178

Index of Saints and Religious Quotes

Blessed Mother Teresa of Calcutta :: x
St. John of the Cross :: xii
Blessed Contardo Ferrini :: 2
St. Francis de Sales :: 4
St. Francis of Assisi :: 4

CHAPTER 1
How and Why People Pray

St. John of Damascus :: 5
Pope Francis :: 6
St. Augustine :: 13
Victor Hugo :: 13
St. Thérèse of Lisieux :: 18
John Henry Cardinal Newman :: 22
St. John Vianney :: 24

CHAPTER 2
Spiritual Motivations and Preparations

St. John of Damascus :: 28
St. Teresa of Avila :: 33
St. Edith Stein :: 35
St. Anselm :: 38

St. John of the Cross :: 38
St. Vincent de Paul :: 40
St. Vincent de Paul :: 42
St. Francis of Assisi :: 43
St. Ignatius of Loyola :: 44
St. Antonius :: 46
St. Bernard :: 46
St. Thomas Aquinas :: 50
Thomas Merton :: 51
St. Zeno :: 51
St. John Berchmans :: 51

CHAPTER 3
A Lifetime of Praying

St. John Paul II :: 53
St. Augustine :: 60
St. Catherine of Siena :: 64
St. Paul :: 64
St. Monica :: 66
Blessed Alexandrina Maria da Costa :: 94
Blessed Mother Teresa of Calcutta :: 97
St. John of the Cross :: 103
Cardinal Timothy Dolan :: 103

CHAPTER 4
Inspirations and Beliefs

St. Ignatius of Loyola :: 105
St. John of the Cross :: 109
St. Ignatius of Loyola :: 109

Index of Saints and Religious Quotes

Mother Mary Angelica :: 110
Blessed Fulton Sheen :: 110
St. John Paul II :: 110
St. Catherine of Siena :: 114
Cardinal Terence Cooke :: 115
St. Paul :: 115
St. Augustine :: 116
St. Jerome :: 116
St. Mary Euphrasia :: 116
St. Augustine :: 117
St. Bernard :: 118
St. Brother Andre Besette :: 118
Blessed Mother Teresa of Calcutta :: 119
Father Peter of Prague :: 119
St. Ambrose :: 120
St. Augustine :: 120
St. Faustina :: 120
St. Thérèse of Lisieux :: 120
St. John Paul II :: 121
Tevye (Fiddler on the Roof) :: 121
St. John Paul II :: 122
St. Teresa of Avila :: 122
St. Cyprian :: 125
St. John Vianney :: 126
St. Louis de Montfort :: 126
St. Polycarp :: 126
St. Teresa of Avila :: 131
Blessed Mother Teresa of Calcutta :: 131
Pope Francis :: 132

St. Catherine of Siena :: 136
St. Nicholas of Tolentino :: 138
St. Augustine :: 141
Pope St. John XXIII :: 141

CHAPTER 5
Spiritual Observations and Resources

St. Peter Eymard :: 147
St. John of the Cross :: 148
St. Catherine Laboure :: 148
St. Augustine :: 148
Blessed Fulton Sheen :: 150
St. Louis de Montfort :: 156
St. Dominic and Blessed Alan de la Roche :: 157
Sister Faustina :: 159
St. Margaret Mary Alacoque :: 168
Fr. Joseph Mary Wolfe, MFVA :: 172
Mother Teresa of Calcutta :: 172
Father Patrick Peyton :: 173
Pope Emeritus Benedict XVI :: 173
St. Anne and St. Joachim :: 175
Elizabeth and Zachary :: 178
Deacon William Steltemeier :: 183

 **About Leonine Publishers**

Leonine Publishers LLC makes fine Catholic literature available to Catholics throughout the English-speaking world. Leonine Publishers offers an innovative "hybrid" approach to book publication that helps authors as well as readers. Please visit our web site at www.leoninepublishers.com to learn more about us. Browse our online bookstore to find more solid Catholic titles to uplift, challenge, and inspire.

Our patron and namesake is Pope Leo XIII, a prudent, yet uncompromising pope during the stormy years at the close of the 19th century. Please join us as we ask his intercession for our family of readers and authors.

Do you have a book inside you? Visit our web site today. Leonine Publishers accepts manuscripts from Catholic authors like you. If your book is selected for publication, you will have an active part in the production process. This book is an example of our growing selection of literature for the busy Catholic reader of the 21st century.

www.leoninepublishers.com

www.ingramcontent.com/pod-product-compliance
Lightning Source LLC
Chambersburg PA
CBHW061431040426
42450CB00007B/992